# ANABAPTIST
# ESSENTIALS

**PRAISE FOR PALMER BECKER**

"The theologian Palmer Becker has a lovely phrase to describe the Mennonite way. . . . It's hard to explain to an outsider how seriously the Mennonites take these three things: Jesus, community, and reconciliation."
—**Malcolm Gladwell**, *on* Revisionist History *podcast*

**PRAISE FOR *ANABAPTIST ESSENTIALS***

"*Anabaptist Essentials* goes deeper into the themes Becker developed in *What is an Anabaptist Christian?* That booklet was widely distributed and has impacted Anabaptist churches around the world. *Anabaptist Essentials* gives a welcome expansion, encouraging further study and spiritual growth."
—**Linda Shelly**, *director for Latin America, Mennonite Mission Network*

"Palmer Becker's *Anabaptist Essentials* illuminates profound Christian values and principles that are not taken seriously by traditional churches but are

indispensable for genuine Christianity. This book provides invaluable resources for those who continue to
seek the original vision of God's kingdom."
—**KyongJung Kim**, *Northeast Asia representative,
Mennonite World Conference*

"*Anabaptist Essentials* is a significant contribution
for those wishing to be engaged in the mission of
the church. It is very accessible and well organized,
gracious in acknowledgment of the contributions of
other denominations, and offers excellent discussion
questions, all in a voice that is invitational and
winsome."
—**Ron Mathies**, *former executive director, Mennonite
Central Committee*

# ANABAPTIST
# ESSENTIALS

Ten Signs of a Unique Christian Faith

# PALMER BECKER

**Herald Press**

Harrisonburg, Virginia

**Library of Congress Cataloging-in-Publication Data**
Names: Becker, Palmer, 1936- author.
Title: Anabaptist essentials : ten signs of a unique Christian faith /
    Palmer Becker.
Description: Harrisonburg, Virginia : Herald Press, [2017] | Includes
    bibliographical references.
Identifiers: LCCN 2016044370| ISBN 9781513800417 (pbk. : alk. paper)
    | ISBN 9781513801407 (hardcover : alk. paper)
Subjects: LCSH: Anabaptists--Doctrines.
Classification: LCC BX4931.3 .B43 2017 | DDC 284/.3--dc23 LC record
available at https://lccn.loc.gov/2016044370

ANABAPTIST ESSENTIALS
© 2017 by Herald Press, Harrisonburg, Virginia 22802
    All rights reserved.
Library of Congress Control Number: 2016044370
International Standard Book Number: 978-1-5138-0041-7 (paper);
    978-1-5138-0140-7 (hard)
Printed in United States of America
Cover and interior design by Merrill Miller
Interior images by Cynthia Friesen Coyle

For orders or information, call 1-800-245-7894 or visit
www.HeraldPress.com.

21 20 19 18 17        10 9 8 7 6 5 4 3 2 1

*Dedicated to my Anabaptist forebears,*

*who lived and died for their faith.*

# Contents

**Introduction** . . . . . . . . . . . . . . . . . . . . . . . . . . . . 9

**A Short History of Christianity** . . . . . . . . . . . . . . 15

**Part I:** Jesus Is the Center of Our Faith

    1 Christianity Is Discipleship . . . . . . . . . . . . . . 29

    2 Scripture Is Interpreted through Jesus . . . . . . . 39

    3 Jesus Is Lord . . . . . . . . . . . . . . . . . . . . . . . . 53

**Part II:** Community Is the Center of Our Life

    4 Forgiveness Is Essential for Community . . . . . . 67

    5 God's Will Is Discerned in Community . . . . . . . 81

    6 Members Are Held Accountable . . . . . . . . . . . 95

**Part III:** Reconciliation Is the Center of Our Work

    7 Individuals Are Reconciled to God . . . . . . . . . 111

    8 Members Are Reconciled to Each Other . . . . . 125

    9 Conflicts in the World Are Reconciled . . . . . . . 137

**Conclusions**

    10 The Holy Spirit's Work Is Essential . . . . . . . . 157

    11 Concluding Reflections on Anabaptist
       Essentials . . . . . . . . . . . . . . . . . . . . . . . . . 169

*Notes* . . . . . . . . . . . . . . . . . . . . . . . . . . . . . . 175

*The Author* . . . . . . . . . . . . . . . . . . . . . . . . . . . 183

# Introduction

**I** **WAS INVITED** to give the keynote address at a conference in Hesston, Kansas, on the topic of "making disciples." It was to focus on how we share our faith from an Anabaptist perspective. Three words came to mind: Jesus, community, and reconciliation. I then expanded those three words to three short sentences that have become widely used and memorable: Jesus is the center of our faith. Community is the center of our life. Reconciliation is the center of our work. Those three sentences are core values that were expanded into the keynote address, then into a twenty-four-page booklet called *What Is an Anabaptist Christian?* Now what started as three words has turned into this book, *Anabaptist Essentials*.

Early Anabaptists lived those three values even if it meant death. Those values were convictions for which they had a passion. They cause me to ask, "What are the convictions and values for which we today are willing to suffer and die?"

In this book I suggest how those values might be understood and practiced today. I write from a North American context but with deep appreciation for what I have learned through numerous teaching assignments in Southeast Asia, the Middle East, and South America. I welcome responses and conversations about how these ten perspectives are being experienced or seen differently in other cultures and places.

Anabaptist Christians hold many beliefs in common with other believers. We believe in a personal three-in-one God who is both holy and merciful. We believe in salvation by grace through repentance and faith, in the humanity and divinity of Jesus, and in the inspiration and authority of Scripture. We believe in the power of the Holy Spirit and in the church as the body of Christ. But Anabaptists tend to hold these basic convictions somewhat differently than other Christians. While these variations may seem small, they make a big difference in how the Christian faith is perceived and practiced.

Anabaptists have often downplayed differences with other believers and highlighted similarities. This is as it should be. Yet this quest for unity has also muted many of the unique qualities and strengths that the Anabaptist tradition might offer to the wider church. Just as there are insights to be learned from a study of the Christian faith from a Catholic, Lutheran, or Baptist viewpoint, so there are unique qualities to be learned from those who practice the Christian faith from an Anabaptist point of view. Each expression of the Christian faith has something to offer the other parts.

In this book I unapologetically describe ten ways in which Anabaptist Christians are uniquely different from many, or even most, Christians. By "uniquely different" I do not mean to imply that Anabaptists are better or that others are wrong. I am simply saying that Anabaptist Christians have something to add to others' understanding of the Christian faith. Imagine an interfaith potluck dinner, with these ten viewpoints the dishes that Anabaptist Christians have to put on the table. As each group contributes its unique perspectives, we all become stronger. The goal of this book is to strengthen Anabaptist faith without becoming competitive or negative toward other views.

I recognize that some of the ways of viewing the Christian faith which were unique and essential to early Anabaptist Christians are now common and taken for granted by many other Christians. However, some beliefs and practices will still seem challenging or perplexing to persons of other traditions.

The three core values upon which this book is built are not new. They are rooted in the person and ministry of Jesus Christ and were basic to the early church. In 1943, Harold S. Bender, president of the American Society of Church History, interpreted these three core values in a statement called "The Anabaptist Vision."[1] He explained that Anabaptist believers see Christianity as *discipleship*, the church as a *brotherhood*, and Christian practice as *an ethic of love and nonresistance*.

While programs and goals may change, business executives counsel that "the unique core values that bring an organization or movement into being should not be changed."[2] They are said to be "sacred." In this book, I defend these core values as essential to the Christian faith and central to what it means to be an Anabaptist Christian.

The first core value, "Jesus is the center of our faith," is discussed in chapters 1, 2, and 3. This value invites us to follow Jesus in daily life, interpret the Scriptures through the eyes of Jesus, and see Jesus as our final authority.

The second core value, "Community is the center of our life," is explored in chapters 4, 5, and 6. This value maintains that horizontal forgiveness is essential for community, that the giving and receiving of counsel is necessary for discerning the will of God, and that small groups are the basic unit of the church.

The third core value, "Reconciliation is the center of our work," is examined in chapters 7, 8, and 9. This value speaks to how individuals are reconciled to God, how members are reconciled to each other, and how believers are to function as peacebuilders in a broken world.

Chapters 10 and 11 conclude the book. Chapter 10 maintains that the early Anabaptists were the charismatic movement of the Reformation and that the work of the Holy Spirit is essential for the actualization and practice of the Christian faith. Chapter 11 allows the reader to personally reflect on the main points of this book.

The three core values with their unifying center may be depicted as shown in the illustration.

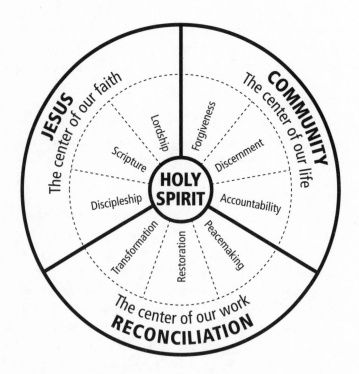

The brevity of this book is both its strength and its weakness. I have tended to emphasize the positive contributions of the early Anabaptists while failing to adequately lift up the strengths of other faith traditions. My purpose in doing so is to focus on the ideals of the Anabaptist movement so they can be discussed and applied in today's settings. I will be the first to admit that the Anabaptists were not always right and didn't always practice what they preached.

Followers of Jesus can believe deeply, and simultaneously relate warmly and openly with those who have other convictions. We all need to fellowship, think, and work together whenever and wherever possible. As we think and work together, we are challenged to share our perspectives and convictions with each other. While we need to guard against any union that would sap our spiritual vitality, we need to affirm what others are doing in the spirit of Christ. Where we do disagree—whether as individuals, churches, or denominations—it is essential that we do so in a spirit of love. A spirit of love includes listening carefully to each other while sharing with passion the truths we have found to be helpful.

In writing these chapters, I have received particular help from a presentation by Jeff Wright in Los Angeles and from authors Stuart Murray, Alfred Neufeld, John Roth, and C. Arnold Snyder.[3] The *Confession of Faith in a Mennonite Perspective*, adopted in 1995 by Mennonite Church USA and Mennonite Church Canada, was a basic frame of reference.[4] Barb Draper assisted in preparing the questions for discussion. Cynthia Friesen Coyle drew the illustrative images, and Mark Weising, Ally Siebert, and Mandy Witmer helped with research and initial editing. Valerie Weaver-Zercher, as book editor, gave wonderful counsel throughout the process. To them, and to Ardys, my patient wife, I owe a sincere debt of gratitude.

—*Palmer Becker*

# A Short History of Christianity

**THE EARLY CHURCH** was born on the day of Pentecost when the Holy Spirit came upon a group of Jesus' followers gathered in an upper room in Jerusalem (see Acts 1:12-14; 2:1-4). On that day the apostle Peter stood before the crowds and pleaded for the people to repent of their wrong loyalties, words, and actions and to accept Jesus as the center of their faith. Approximately three thousand were added to the church that day (see Acts 2:38-41).

For the first 250 years, Christians were seen as a people who lived visibly new lives in obedience to Jesus, whom they had accepted as their teacher, Savior, and Lord. Many called followers of Jesus "people of the Way" (Acts 9:2; 19:9, 23; 24:14, 22).

According to the book of Acts, they were transformed people who met in each other's homes, shared their possessions freely, and as time passed, welcomed new believers regardless of race, class, or place of origin.

## What changes came to the Christian faith?

Unfortunately, during the next few centuries, so many changes came to the Christian faith that it became like a different religion.[1] While most Christians have rejoiced that this was a time when heavy persecution ended and the church suddenly grew to include nearly all of northern Africa, the Middle East, and Europe, Anabaptists have viewed this time as the "fall" of the church.

Two men became symbols of a major shift from original Christianity to what has been called Christendom, or the era and domain of imperial religion. One was a politician, the other was a theologian.

**Constantine**, the politician, was emperor of the Roman Empire from 306 to 337 CE.[2] During the Battle of the Milvian Bridge in 312, he claimed to have seen a vision of the cross with Greek words above it: "In this sign, conquer." He won the battle and, as a result, stopped the persecution of Christians and allowed the Christian faith to become a recognized religion of the Roman Empire.

In time, Constantine became not only the head of the growing Roman Empire but also the head of the expanding church. Millions of people, including people of wealth and influence, became "Christian" during this period. Further, new members were gained through military conquests as "Christian" emperors forced conquered people to convert to Christianity, even if those people did not have a desire to do so. As a result, instead of the church being in the world, too often the world came into the church.

From an Anabaptist point of view, the church lost many of its essential qualities and characteristics. Stuart Murray observes that Christendom "marginalized, spiritualized, and domesticated Jesus." He goes on to say that in Christendom "the teaching of Jesus is watered down, privatized, and explained away. Jesus is worshiped as a remote kingly figure or a romanticized personal savior."[3]

Constantine the Great          Augustine of Hippo

JEAN-CHRISTOPHE BENOIST

In earlier years, believers in Christ had met together in fellowship groups. Now, with the expansion of the church, they met in large church structures that had been commissioned by Constantine and those who followed him. Instead of emphasizing the need for believers to follow Jesus in daily life, prominence was given to religious doctrine, mystical experience, and forgiveness of sin. Little emphasis was placed on believers being inwardly transformed to think, feel, and act like their Lord. As a result, people came to be judged more by the uniformity of their beliefs than by the lives they lived.

**Augustine** (354–430 CE), the theologian, rose to prominence about one hundred years after Constantine came to power.[4] Like Constantine, he also had a profound conversion experience, and some today would call him the greatest theologian of the Western church. However, because of his teaching, church leaders began to focus more on Christ's death than on his life. Anselm, a later theologian (1033–1109), especially influenced Christendom to focus on the mystery of Christ's death for the sins of the world rather than on Christ as a servant-leader to be followed. Instead of saying "Jesus is the center of our faith," followers of Augustine and Anselm tended to say, "Christ's death is the center of our faith."

For the first 250 years of the church's existence, followers of Christ were a persecuted minority who worshiped in secret or under pressure in close, intimate communities. Now, under Christendom, they met in ornate buildings financed by government and church taxation. Whereas, previously, new converts had undergone significant training, received adult baptism, and joined committed fellowships, now individuals were baptized as infants, and all citizens (except Jews) were considered to be Christian. Largely lost was the sense of the church as the body of Christ that functioned as a family.

Members of the early church had regularly shared their faith with their neighbors and had taken the gospel to the outer corners of the known world. Now the task of reconciling people to God and to each other was greatly diminished. Almost all early church Christians had rejected military service. Now Christians, like everyone else, were expected to serve in the military.

During the Middle Ages, most people believed that ordinary individuals could not live as Jesus had lived. Although religious leaders placed more and more emphasis on prayer and the forgiveness of sin, morality among both the clergy and the common people fell to low levels. True discipleship could still be found in the monastic movement, but for a thousand years the majority of Christians lived under this changed religion called Christendom. The Islamic faith, in part, rose up as a correction to fallen Christianity.

## What did the Protestant Reformation accomplish?

Between 1200 and 1550 CE, a number of concerned leaders began to realize there were serious inadequacies in their practice of the Christian faith. One such reformer was Martin Luther (1483–1546), a German monk who was thoroughly

LUCAS CRANACH D.Ä.

Martin Luther

schooled in Augustinian theology. Ulrich Zwingli, a Swiss pastor (1484–1531), and John Calvin, an influential French theologian (1509–64), were others. They came forward to bring correction to the Christian faith and renewal to the church.

The practices of priests and popes, who offered forgiveness from sin and release from purgatory on the basis of good works and the selling of indulgences, were especially offensive to Luther. On October 31, 1517, in an attempt to call for public debate about these practices, Luther nailed a list of ninety-five theses to a church door in Wittenberg, Germany. This act launched the great Protestant Reformation, from which the Anabaptist movement emerged.[5]

Luther and other Protestant leaders sought to restore the church to its original core values and purposes as described in the Scriptures. They separated themselves from the powers, traditions, and rituals of the church's hierarchy in Rome. In their meetings they preached salvation by grace, justification by faith, and the priesthood of all believers. They believed that the church existed wherever the Word of God was proclaimed truthfully and the sacraments were administered correctly.

In 1524, the peasants of Germany, eager to free themselves not only from the dictates of Rome but also from the unjust practices of the feudal system, began a series of uprisings against their cruel lords. In the interest of maintaining order and to halt the chaos, Luther and Zwingli sided with the political authorities and feudal lords. In so doing, they unintentionally and unfortunately forged a new alliance between church and state.

The uprisings prevented Luther and Zwingli from implementing many of their intended reforms. They, together with most other leaders of the Reformation, reverted to the structures initiated by Constantine and to the theology drafted by Augustine. This meant returning to the state church as the polity of the church, to the bishop's seat as the structure of the church, to infant baptism as the introductory rite into the church, to the use of the sword by government as the tool for discipline, and to the Ten Commandments as the primary frame of reference for ethics. In many ways, little change had been accomplished.

## How did the Anabaptist faith begin?

During the height of the Protestant Reformation, several of Ulrich Zwingli's students, including Conrad Grebel (1498–1526), Felix Manz (1498–1527), and George Blaurock (1491–1529), gathered regularly for Bible study, discussion, and prayer in Zurich, Switzerland. Hans Hut (1490–1527), Hans Denck (1495–1527), Pilgram Marpeck (d. 1556), and Jacob Hutter (1500–1536) began similar practices in South Germany and Moravia. A few years later, Melchior Hoffman (1495–1543), Menno Simons (1496–1561), Obbe Philips (1500–1568), and his brother Dirk Philips (1504–1568) brought new thinking to the Netherlands.

These individuals, each in his own way, rediscovered an active, living Jesus. Had you asked these students about their beliefs and practices, they probably would have agreed with the first disciples in saying "Jesus Christ is the center of our faith. Community is the center of our life. Reconciliation is the center of our work."

They came to believe that the church should be composed of those who make an adult confession of faith and who commit themselves to following Jesus in daily life. On January 21, 1525, Grebel, Manz, and Blaurock baptized each other. Thus began the Anabaptist (literally "rebaptizers") movement.

These early Anabaptists broke completely with the concepts of Christendom held by both Catholic and Protestant leaders and institutions. They insisted the church existed not only when the Word was preached truthfully and the sacraments were administered properly but also when its members led revitalized lives of public obedience to Jesus Christ. For the Anabaptists, faith by itself was insufficient for either salvation or community. Only those willing to repent of false loyalties and be obedient to Christ in daily life could be members. Love was the chief mark of the church—a love that expressed itself in mutual care for each other, for those around them, and even for their enemies.

Dozens of Anabaptist groups soon sprang up, and within two years the numbers grew to about two thousand members. In 1527, their leaders met in Schleitheim, Switzerland, where they drafted a common confession of faith that included statements about baptism, communion, separation from evil, responsibilities of pastors, speaking the truth, and refusal to participate in violence.[6] Anabaptist believers quickly became known for their exemplary lives. In public trials, men and women who did not drink to excess, curse, or abuse their workers or families were often suspected of being Anabaptist—and thus subject to persecution and even death.[7]

Somewhat later, Menno Simons, a former Catholic priest in the Netherlands, joined the Anabaptists and became an itinerant preacher. He gathered believers together and met with groups for Bible study and discussion in homes and in other secret places.[8] After the defeat of radical extremists who had taken over the city of Münster, he wrote extensive works

Menno Simons

HUGO BÜRKNER

and was effective in bringing unity to much of the Anabaptist movement. Thanks to Menno's visits and influence, members of the various groups became known first as Mennists and later as Mennonites.

While these first Anabaptist/Mennonite Christians (the terms are often used interchangeably) affirmed the ancient Apostles' Creed and belief in salvation by grace, they became something of a hybrid that was both Catholic and Protestant. In describing them, author and theologian Walter Klaassen has gone so far as to write *Anabaptism: Neither Catholic nor Protestant.*[9] In contrast to Catholics, Anabaptists had no holy words, no sacred things, no holy places, and no sacred persons. In contrast to Protestants, they preferred to think of themselves as being born again and transformed rather than as being justified by faith through grace.

The Anabaptists also spoke more about the Holy Spirit than did the majority of either Catholic or Protestant leaders. For these reasons, they came to be seen as a third variety of Christianity. Some have called them the "left wing" of the Protestant Reformation. Author Paul Lederach has referred to the Anabaptist movement as "a third way."[10]

In their small groups and church gatherings, the early Anabaptists continued their rediscovery of Jesus and the ways of his first disciples. Living according to the Sermon on the Mount—as made possible by the empowering presence of the Holy Spirit—was the ideal for all members. Some of their favorite Scriptures included Hebrews 12:2: "Looking to Jesus the pioneer and perfecter of our faith," and 1 Corinthians 3:11: "No one can lay any foundation other than the one that has been laid; that foundation is Jesus Christ." Hans Denck, an early Anabaptist, stated it clearly when he said, "No one can truly know Christ unless they follow after him in daily life, and no one can follow Christ in daily life unless they truly know him."[11]

## How has Anabaptism grown?

Early Anabaptist Christians might be seen as a unique strain of wheat. The original unique seeds grew quickly. Within two decades, the movement had spread to every province of Europe—as far as Scandinavia to the north and Greece to the south. In some areas, Anabaptists outnumbered Lutherans.[12]

Because of their views on baptism and the church, which were considered heretical, Anabaptists came to be persecuted by both Catholic and Protestant leaders. Intense persecution, which lasted for one hundred years, caused the early Anabaptist Christians to withdraw into separate communities or to flee to Moravia, Poland, North America, and the Ukraine, where it was more safe to practice their beliefs. For more than four hundred years, these safe communities were like a jar of inbred seeds set on a shelf.

Early in the twentieth century, and especially during and after World War II, great changes took place. Young people left their safe communities to go to war, to Civilian Public Service camps, or to new jobs in the cities. Others went into mission work in Asia, Africa, and South America, where they encountered new challenges and engaged with people of different faiths and cultures. It was as if the jar containing unique

Anabaptist seed had been knocked off the mantel. It crashed to the ground, and its seeds were spread to all parts of the world. They now needed to grow and produce new seed, or else they would die. Thankfully, many of those seeds have taken root in new places, mixed with other strains, and become a highly sought-after hybrid.

Mennonite Christians, who stem from the Anabaptist movement, stand in this tradition, as do Amish, Hutterite, and Brethren in Christ believers. Today, these believers number approximately two million and can be found in more than one hundred countries around the world.

In "The Anabaptist Vision," Harold S. Bender claimed, "The great principles of freedom of conscience, separation of church and state, and voluntarism in religion, . . . so essential to democracy, ultimately are derived from the Anabaptists of the Reformation period, who for the first time clearly enunciated them and challenged the Christian world to follow them in practice."[13]

How can we continue to learn from this third way of understanding the Christian faith? What qualities of the Christian faith can be learned? In what ways are those qualities essential rather than just important? In the chapters ahead, I will share, from my North American context and understanding, ten signs of a unique Christian faith. I commend this faith to you for dialogue and joyful practice.

## Questions for reflection and discussion

1. Is it possible to strengthen Anabaptist faith without becoming competitive or hostile toward other traditions? In what ways have you engaged in helpful dialogue with persons of other denominations or faiths?

2. Reflect on the following contrasts between the early church and Christendom. Can we have both, or must we choose?

| The early church emphasized: | Christendom emphasized: |
| --- | --- |
| The life, teachings, death, and resurrection of Jesus | The mystery, death, and resurrection of Jesus |
| Meeting in homes | Meeting in cathedrals |
| Ministry and evangelism | Doctrine and organization |
| Baptism of adults | Baptism of infants |
| Living at peace | Going to war when required to do so |

3. How is worshiping in a small house church a different experience from worshiping in a large, ornate cathedral? What are the advantages and disadvantages of these two settings for worship?

4. What do you think of Walter Klaassen's statement that Anabaptism is neither Catholic nor Protestant?

**Part I**

# Jesus
## Is the Center of Our Faith

# ONE

# Christianity Is Discipleship

*If any want to become my followers, let them deny*
*themselves and take up their cross daily and follow me.*
*Luke 9:23*

**H**OW IS ONE to answer the question, "What is Christianity?" While that question sounds ultrasimple, it can be answered in a variety of ways. While all Christian traditions affirm that Jesus is central, each has a tendency to interpret this in its own way. In this chapter, I seek to describe how Jesus and the first disciples understood the Christian faith, and how several contemporary traditions view it. We must begin with Jesus and the early church.

## How did early Christians understand Christianity?

For three years the first followers of Jesus lived, ate, and worked with Jesus. They observed how he cared for the poor, healed those who were ill, gave sight to the blind, related to the marginalized, forgave sinners, taught the multitudes, and responded to enemies. During these years of compassionate, Spirit-filled ministry—and through Jesus' subsequent death, resurrection, and the giving of his Holy Spirit—discipleship became central to those first followers.

The first followers of Jesus were called disciples. While that is what the followers of any great teacher were called, Christ's disciples went further than simply being students of Jesus. Their creed was "Jesus Christ is Lord" (Philippians 2:11). This commitment needed to be lived within a hostile environment in which everyone was required to pledge their supreme allegiance to Caesar and his dominant order.

For the disciples, ultimate allegiance belonged to Jesus. He was inaugurating God's social order. This order and the relationships in it functioned as the continuing body of Christ. The task of the disciples and all subsequent followers was to continue what Jesus had begun. They followed his nature and style in daily life.

To live in joyful obedience to Jesus required something supernatural. It required followers to be "born again" (John 3:3 KJV). To be born again meant to make a new start. Disciples needed to repent, or turn from, following other lords or loyalties and to commit themselves to following Jesus as their living Lord. On the day of Pentecost they received the Holy Spirit, which gave them the insight and power needed to live as Jesus had lived.

Christ's final instruction to those disciples was to make more disciples, and that is what they did. Even when persecution made it difficult, those first Christians shared throughout the Roman Empire their understandings of Jesus and what it meant to follow him. The early followers became known as "people of the Way" because they were living in the way of Jesus.

## How do today's believers understand Christianity?

Following are four ways in which people of different traditions answer the question "What is Christianity?" These viewpoints are listed in the illustration.

**The Christian faith**

## Is Christianity a set of beliefs?

Believers in liturgical churches tend to place their emphasis on God the Father and on a right set of beliefs. They teach the basic beliefs of the Christian faith in confirmation or membership classes and repeat the Apostles' Creed each Sunday. Some might go so far as to say, "Christianity is believing."

Beliefs are important, and we can all learn from those in liturgical churches who have a high regard for creeds and statements of faith. The apostle Paul gives support to beliefs by promising early Christians, "If you confess with your lips that Jesus is Lord and believe in your heart that God raised him from the dead, you will be saved" (Romans 10:9).

The Christian faith might be seen as a combination of believing, belonging, and behaving.[1] John Wesley (1703–91) identified these parts of Christianity as orthodoxy (right beliefs), orthopathy (right experience), and orthopraxy (right practices).[2]

Followers of Christ become unbalanced when they stress one area of the Christian faith, such as beliefs, at the expense of others. Christians from an Anabaptist perspective affirm that the Christian faith includes a set of beliefs, but they insist that an emphasis on orthodoxy, or right beliefs, needs to be kept in balance with other aspects of the Christian faith, especially that of orthopraxy, or right practice.

## Is Christianity a spiritual experience?

Charismatic and Pentecostal Christians tend to place emphasis on the Holy Spirit and on special spiritual experiences (orthopathos). Christians of this persuasion often testify that they came to faith through a supernatural experience such as being healed, freed from a demon, or guided in some special way. Some would go so far as to say that speaking in tongues is the essential indicator that one is a Christian.

Anabaptists would affirm that spiritual experience is part of the Christian faith. They recognize that Jesus performed supernatural miracles and that early Christians saw the apostles do many signs and wonders (see Acts 2:43). But Anabaptist Christians caution that Christian faith cannot be described as or limited to spiritual experience.

## Is Christianity an experience of forgiveness?

Evangelical Christians stress the sacred experience of being forgiven by God. Some evangelists, after preaching the gospel in a convincing way, invite those who want to become Christians to pray the "sinner's prayer." Some would go so far as to say that one should be able to name the time and place when confession of sin was made and forgiveness was received.

Christians from an Anabaptist perspective affirm that confession of sin and forgiveness are essential for salvation. Jesus began his ministry by saying, "Repent, and believe" (Mark 1:15). But forgiveness of sins is not the sum total of the Christian faith. While praying a sinner's prayer may begin the Christian journey and be seen as the minimum requirement for entrance into heaven, there is more to the Christian faith than forgiveness.

## Is Christianity discipleship?

Anabaptist Christians affirm that Christianity includes beliefs, spiritual experience, and forgiveness. But particular emphasis is placed on following Jesus in daily life. Anabaptist Christians will go so far as to say, "Christianity is discipleship!"

Discipleship means following Jesus in daily life. It calls for living the same kind of life that Jesus lived. Jesus said, "If you continue in my word, you are truly my disciples" (John 8:31). Disciples are joyfully obedient to Jesus Christ because of what he did and continues to do for them.

Just as some traditions might stress right beliefs, right experience, or right forgiveness at the expense of discipleship, Anabaptists are in danger of stressing right practice (orthopraxy) at the expense of ignoring other aspects of faith. Renowned Anglican theologian J. I. Packer once shared with me, "I get frustrated that Anabaptists don't seem to take time to think. They are always *doing* things! But then, I must admit that they are doing more than we."[3]

Discipleship insists that faith and obedience must be held together. Faith requires obedience, and obedience requires faith. James insists that if there is no obedience, there is no faith, saying, "Faith by itself, if it has no works, is dead" (James 2:17).

Jesus himself said, "Not everyone who says to me, 'Lord, Lord,' will enter the kingdom of heaven, but only the one who does the will of my Father in heaven. On that day many will say to me, 'Lord, Lord, did we not prophesy in your name, and cast out demons in your name, and do many deeds of power in your name?' Then, I will declare to them, 'I never knew you; go away from me, you evildoers'" (Matthew 7:21-23).

## How did early Anabaptists come to this faith?

Early Anabaptists, through Bible study, discussion, and prayer, rediscovered a living Jesus. They found that his life, priorities, and commands were clearly written in the Gospels. They rooted their obedience to Jesus in the Sermon on the Mount. The Holy Spirit reminded them who he was, what he had said, and what he called them to do.

"Jesus is the center of our faith" is the first core value of Anabaptist faith. While other traditions might also say that Jesus is central, Anabaptist Christians have strongly emphasized that obedient following of Jesus, not mere believing, is what makes Jesus central. Adult baptism communicates to family, friends, and a church community that a person is committed to following Jesus in daily life.

The late Doris Janzen Longacre, a Mennonite theologian and the author of the *More-with-Less* cookbook, confirmed this when she wrote, "We can rehearse background facts, share experience, and distill standards to guide future decisions. We can attend workshops and conferences, draw on still more experience, and collect a helpful library, but when we close the books and come home from the discussions, one voice still speaks in the silence. For Christians it is the call to obedience."[4]

Early Anabaptists were encouraged by the words of Jesus, who said, "Come, you that are blessed by my Father, inherit the kingdom prepared for you from the foundation of the world; for I was hungry and you gave me food, I was thirsty and you gave me something to drink, I was a stranger and you welcomed me, I was naked and you gave me clothing, I was sick and you took care of me, I was in prison and you visited me" (Matthew 25:34-36).

Jesus ends his famous Sermon on the Mount, which serves as the manifesto of the Christian faith, by saying, "Everyone then who hears these words of mine and acts on them will be like a wise man who built his house on rock. The rain fell, the floods came, and the winds blew and beat on that house, but it did not fall, because it had been founded on rock. And everyone who hears these words of mine and does not act on them will be like a foolish man who built his house on sand. The rain fell, and the floods came, and the winds blew and beat against that house, and it fell—and great was its fall!" (Matthew 7:24-27).

## How do we understand discipleship?

If the essence of Christianity is discipleship, or following Jesus in daily life, it is important for us to understand clearly what this means. Christians in an Anabaptist stream believe that when a person comes to an age of accountability—that is, when a person is old enough to become responsible for his or her decisions—that individual must make a decision, or a series of decisions, to turn from other loyalties and ways of living to following Jesus Christ. "It is not enough to know about Jesus and salvation," writes Bible and ministry professor Michele Hershberger in *God's Story, Our Story*. "It's not enough to be able to explain what everything means in the Story and how it all fits together. Knowing all this, you must make a choice. Will you follow Jesus? Will you say yes to him?"[5]

Such a decision may mean making a new start both personally and in the context of a new group. When Jesus said, "You must be born again" (John 3:7 KJV), he was referring to something more than "being saved." While being saved often means being delivered from bad habits or being saved from going to hell at the end of this life, being born again means beginning to live in a new way in this life. Being born again causes one's thoughts, attitudes, and actions to be transformed, and enables one to make a new start.

My father, whose first language was German, understood Christianity as *nachfolge Christi*, which means "following Jesus." When it came to baptism, he was perplexed by the question "Are you saved?" His answer was, "I am a follower of Jesus." He was baptized upon that confession of faith.

Professor of pastoral care and counseling David Augsburger notes that Anabaptists, from their beginnings in 1525 to the present, have pursued a dream. This dream suggests that:

- It is reasonable to follow Jesus Christ daily, radically, totally in life.

- It is practical to obey the Sermon on the Mount, and the whole New Testament, literally, honestly, sacrificially.

- It is thinkable to practice the way of reconciling love in human conflicts and warfare, nondefensively and nonresistantly.

- It is possible to confess Jesus as Lord above all nationalism, racism, or materialism.

- It is feasible to build a communal church of brothers and sisters who are voluntary, disciplined, and mutually committed to each other in Christ.

- Life can be lived simply, following the Jesus way in lifestyle, in possessions, and in service.[6]

## What is essential to Anabaptist Christianity?

Understanding that "Christianity is discipleship!" is essential to understanding Christianity from an Anabaptist perspective. It means continuing to do in our day what Jesus began doing in 30 CE!

Discipleship is the result of being transformed through an active relationship with Jesus Christ. It is an exciting way to view and live the Christian faith.

"Can we walk together with other Christians?" asks César García, general secretary of Mennonite World Conference, an international association of Anabaptist churches. "Yes . . . but not merely because we share a set of theoretical doctrines that we must confess intellectually. Instead, we share convictions and relationships that are the fruit of our walk with Christ, as did our forebears of the sixteenth century."[7]

Just as there are several ways of answering the question "What is Christianity?" so there are several ways of answering the question "How do we interpret Scripture?" We will explore those ways in the next chapter.

## Questions for reflection and discussion

1. How would you answer the question "What is Christianity?"

2. Reflect on these contrasting views that can be found within the Christian faith:

| Many Christians emphasize: | Anabaptist Christians emphasize: |
|---|---|
| Christianity is primarily about beliefs. | Beliefs are important but not primary. |
| Christianity is primarily about spiritual experience. | Spiritual experience is important but not primary. |
| Christianity is primarily about forgiveness. | Forgiveness is important but not primary. |
| Christianity is primarily about eternal salvation. | Christianity is primarily about following Jesus in daily life. |

3. What practical difference will it make when a person affirms that "Christianity is discipleship"?

4. In what way is Paul and Silas's statement "Believe in the Lord Jesus" (Acts 16:31 NIV) the same as "Follow the Lord Jesus in everyday life"?

# TWO

# Scripture Is Interpreted through Jesus

*Long ago God spoke to our ancestors in many and
various ways by the prophets, but in these last days
he has spoken to us by a Son.*

*Hebrews 1:1-2*

**HOW ARE WE** to interpret the Scriptures? Differences
of interpretation are often at the root of misunderstandings and divisions between believers. "The Bible has become a
battleground on which current cultural wars are being fought,"
grieves Sara Wenger Shenk, president of Anabaptist Mennonite
Biblical Seminary. "Our church is being pulled apart because
of wrongheaded ways of reading and interpreting the Bible."[1]

In this chapter, I explain four approaches to interpreting
the Scriptures. We will then explore how Anabaptist Christians

have come to understand and obey the Scriptures somewhat differently than many or even most other Christians.

## How did the Scriptures come to us?

Beginning with Moses and stretching over a period of about fifteen hundred years, more than forty authors, under the guidance of the Holy Spirit, wrote the sixty-six books of the Bible. Some New Testament books were first written fifty, a hundred, or even more years after the birth of Christ. Early Christians had a background in Old Testament scrolls, but basically preached and ministered out of what they and the apostles remembered from the ministry and spirit of Jesus. As time passed, Christian leaders chose the present books of the Bible and developed various ways of interpreting them. For example, Augustine developed a complicated fourfold approach to biblical interpretation, suggesting that each passage of Scripture has four potential meanings. These are:

1. Literal: What the passage says about the past

2. Allegorical: What the passage says about Christ

3. Moral: What the passage says about how to live

4. Prophetic: What the passage says about humans' ultimate fate

Within these parameters, interpreting Scripture became very difficult, so for more than a thousand years, Bible study was left to educated monks and scholars who mostly interpreted Scriptures according to tradition. Then, during the Reformation of the 1500s, Martin Luther and others translated the Bible into the common languages of the people. Between 1516 and 1550, nearly thirty new translations of the Bible appeared in Europe.[2] With the invention of the printing press, it suddenly became possible for ordinary believers to have access to the Scriptures. Eager readers purchased the translations as fast as they appeared!

Luther preached *sola scriptura*, which means "by Scripture alone." While he held that only the Bible should determine faith and life, he retained many traditional ways of interpreting the Bible and therefore did not give full freedom to religious thought.

Like other Christians, early Anabaptists believed the Scriptures were inspired and "useful for teaching, for reproof, for correction, and for training in righteousness" (2 Timothy 3:16). They had many discussions with other reformers on how to interpret the Scriptures.

In recent times, as in the Reformation, we have been inundated with translations and new forms of communication. In the midst of new availability of the Scriptures, four methods or approaches to interpreting the Scriptures have come into common use: (1) flat, or literal; (2) dispensational; (3) spiritualized Christ-centered; and (4) ethical Christ-centered. Following is a brief explanation of these approaches.

## What is the flat Bible approach?

Many Christians believe all Scripture is equal in value or authority. They lay the Bible flat and make little distinction between the Old and New Testaments. For example, what Moses said in Deuteronomy is on par with what Jesus said in the Sermon on the Mount. This view is called the "flat Bible" approach to biblical interpretation.

Christians with a flat Bible approach are often quite literalistic in their interpretation. They might say, "I just read the Bible and do what it says." However, since it is not possible to do everything the Bible says, they are selective in what they choose to teach and do. Also, everyone inevitably interprets what they read according to individual understanding shaped by background and context.

### The flat Bible approach

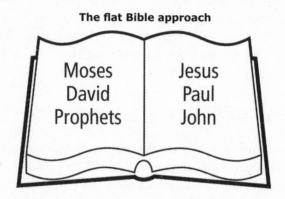

Moses
David
Prophets

Jesus
Paul
John

When flat Bible interpreters encounter political or social issues such as war, capital punishment, or the treatment of deviant people, they often use Old Testament texts as the basis for their belief and action, even when those texts differ from the teachings of Jesus in the New Testament. When they encounter matters of personal ethics, they often go to the epistles. The Gospels get neglected.

When we examine Scripture, it is important to remember that much of what is written is descriptive rather than prescriptive. In other words, the Bible *describes* what the people of the time thought or did but does not necessarily *prescribe* that this is what we are to do today. For this reason, we cannot just "read the Bible and do what it says."

For early Anabaptist Christians, it was not enough for leaders to study only the written Scripture in preparation for teaching and preaching. They needed both Word and Spirit. They got into trouble when they elevated the literal written Word over the Spirit or when they raised the Spirit above the written Word. "Anabaptists taught 'Scripture and Spirit together,'" observes author C. Arnold Snyder.[3] This was in contrast to the "Scripture alone" approach of Luther. It has been said, somewhat crudely, "If you have only the Word, you dry up. If you have only the Spirit, you blow up. But if you have both the Word and the Spirit, you grow up!"[4]

For these reasons, Anabaptist Christians do not believe the flat Bible approach is the best method for interpreting the Scriptures.

## What is the dispensational approach?

The dispensational approach to interpreting the Scriptures was first proposed around 1800 by John Darby, a leader of the Plymouth Brethren. Those who follow this approach believe that God had different wills during various "dispensations," or periods of history. The Scriptures and God's will need to be interpreted according to that period of time.

**The dispensational approach**

As the illustration shows, the four (or more) biblical dispensations include the ages of patriarchal promise, the age of Mosaic Law, the age of the church, and the final millennial age, when Jesus will return to rule on earth.

Dispensationalism gives center stage to the old covenant and the Israelite people instead of to Jesus and the church. It reveres prophecy over just living. As a result, many evangelical and Zionist Christians give more emphasis to prophecy than to biblical justice. This is especially evident in attitudes toward the nation of Israel and its occupation of Palestinian land.

Most unfortunate is that under the dispensational approach, the teachings of Jesus, as found in the Sermon on the Mount, are seen as applicable only for the time that Jesus was on earth and when he will return. Present-day Christians are not expected or encouraged to live according to the Sermon on the Mount.

For these reasons, Anabaptist Christians do not believe the dispensational approach is the best one for interpreting the Scriptures.

## What is the spiritualized Christ-centered approach?

Most Christians affirm a Christ-centered approach to interpreting Scripture, but many spiritualize Jesus. Their understanding of Jesus is largely limited to his sacrificial death on the cross. This approach places great emphasis on the Old Testament Scriptures that they believe look forward to the time when Jesus would give his life as a final sacrifice for the sins of the world and New Testament Scriptures that look back to that event.

Those who employ this narrower spiritualized approach to Jesus run the risk of interpreting some Old Testament Scriptures in ways not intended by the original writers. More seriously, they focus almost entirely on the sacrificial death of Jesus and fail to see that the way Jesus lived and what he stood for were key factors leading to his death. Those who adhere to the spiritualized Christ-centered approach to interpreting the Scriptures generally preach and teach from the Old Testament or the epistles of Paul rather than from the life and teachings of Jesus.

**The spiritualized Christ-centered approach**

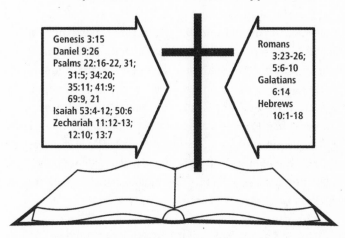

Genesis 3:15
Daniel 9:26
Psalms 22:16-22, 31;
   31:5; 34:20;
   35:11; 41:9;
   69:9, 21
Isaiah 53:4-12; 50:6
Zechariah 11:12-13;
   12:10; 13:7

Romans
   3:23-26;
   5:6-10
Galatians
   6:14
Hebrews
   10:1-18

While Anabaptist Christians affirm the critical importance of Christ's death, we do not believe the spiritualized Christocentric approach is the best method for interpreting the Scriptures. This approach fails to adequately emphasize that the essence of Christian faith lies in following a living Jesus in the context of a Jesus-centered community.

## What is the ethical Christ-centered approach?

A fourth approach to interpreting Scripture maintains that since Jesus is the fullest revelation of God and God's will, he is the key to interpreting the Scriptures. The entire Bible needs to be interpreted through the eyes and nature of Jesus. "At the center of the Bible is Jesus," says Bruxy Cavey, teaching pastor at The Meeting House. "Jesus is at the center of who we are. To get to know Jesus as well as we can, the Sermon on the Mount is a wonderful starting point."[5]

"If all the Scriptures do is introduce me to Jesus Christ," maintains missionary Peter Kehler, "that is enough!" He goes on to say, "The Scriptures do much more, but their greatest contribution is that they introduce us to Jesus Christ who is our Savior and guide."[6]

Why is Jesus given such high priority? Abraham, Moses, David, and the prophets had increasing understandings of God and God's will. They built on each other's understandings and on the additional revelations given to them. In this process, the nature of God and God's will became most clear in Jesus Christ. This is stated succinctly in the book of Hebrews: "Long ago God spoke to our ancestors in many and various ways by the prophets, but in these last days he has spoken to us by a Son . . . [who] is the reflection of God's glory and the exact imprint of God's very being" (Hebrews 1:1-3).

**The ethical Christ-centered approach**

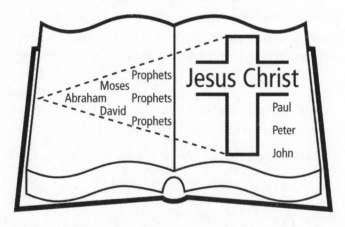

The teachings of Jesus fulfill and sometimes even transcend previous teachings of Scripture. "Jesus interpreted it [the Old Testament] for his own day," says Ervin Stutzman, executive director of Mennonite Church USA. "Jesus [said] 'you have heard

that it was said,' then he quoted an Old Testament passage followed by 'but I tell you,' showing God's better way today. He
claimed the authority to reinterpret those Scriptures by saying
of himself, 'One greater than Moses is here.'"[7]

God continues to reveal himself in our everyday experiences and through Spirit-directed brothers and sisters who
are seeking to follow Jesus in daily life. "God is continually
revealed to humanity," says pastor and mission advocate John
Powell. "Each experience brings us into an understanding of
God's authority and preeminence."[8]

When we want to know what Scripture says about a cer-
tain matter, we go first to the words, example, and spirit of
Jesus. We may go to other Scriptures for further background
and understanding, but our primary guidance comes from
Jesus. When we encounter difficult passages such as those in
the Old Testament that describe violence, we interpret them
in the spirit and nature of Jesus by asking "What would Jesus
say?" or "How would Jesus handle this situation?" Bible professor Marion Bontrager counsels, "If two Scriptures seem to
disagree, let Jesus be the referee!"[9]

In the interpretation of Scripture, Anabaptists have held
together the spiritual and ethical aspects of Christ's life and
ministry. We believe that God and God's will were most clearly
revealed through the wholeness of Jesus Christ. Thus our
ethics come primarily from Christ rather than from the Ten
Commandments and the epistles.

## Does biblical interpretation make a difference?

My late brother and I illustrate how different interpretations
of Scripture cause people to see things differently and can bring
people into conflict. We grew up in the same home, church,
and community. We were almost like twins. After high school,

my brother went to a Bible college, where he was taught to approach the Scriptures from a literalistic, dispensational, and spiritualized Christ-centered point of view. I went to a school where I was taught to interpret the Scriptures from an ethical Christ-centered point of view.

My brother and I came to hold very different views and values in a broad range of areas. When questions emerged about divorce, gun or crime control, immigration, or the war in Iraq, my brother would seek to apply passages from the Old Testament that matched his convictions. I would seek to take my understandings on these topics from the life, teachings, and spirit of Jesus. When the topic of capital punishment was raised, for example, my brother affirmed it on the basis of Old Testament texts such as "If there is serious injury, you are to take life for life, eye for eye, tooth for tooth" (Exodus 21:23-24 NIV). Meanwhile, I looked at Jesus' forgiveness of people who did him harm and asked, "Is ever a person so evil that Jesus would say that person needs to be killed?"

Because my brother had adopted a dispensational approach to interpreting Scripture, we also differed in our understandings of God's will in regard to Israel and Palestine. My brother focused his time and energy on prophecies that he believed spoke to the reestablishment of Israel before Christ's second coming. I, meanwhile, focused more on Christ's first coming and what his teachings say in regard to showing compassion and justice to mistreated peoples such as the Palestinians.

Fortunately, my brother and I were able to love each other even though we had deep misgivings about how the other applied Scripture. We learned that when we could not see eye to eye, we could still speak heart to heart. Too many have failed in this regard.

Gayle Gerber Koontz, professor of theology and ethics at Anabaptist Mennonite Biblical Seminary, notes that Christ-centered interpretations of Scripture move us from the Old Testament's violent destruction of enemies to the Gospels' commandment to treat enemies with love. This approach also moves people from "viewing women simply as property toward . . . an ethic of mutual submission between Christian husbands and wives."[10]

## What about the authority of Scripture?

While the inspiration and trustworthiness of Scripture is important, the matter of authority is even more important. One who has authority has the power to command. Scripture is given authority when we obey its commands, especially the commands of Jesus.

Jesus concluded his ministry by saying, "All authority in heaven and on earth has been given to me" (Matthew 28:18). We give authority to Jesus when we recognize him as our Lord and respond to his commands and wishes. While we give authority to all Scriptures, we interpret and obey them through the words, spirit, and nature of Jesus.

Interpreting the Scriptures from an ethical Christ-centered point of view is another way of affirming that Jesus is Lord. "Christ is the head of the church, ever caring for its good," says Grace Holland, former chair of the Brethren in Christ Board for World Missions. "He will guide our understanding of Scripture to the appropriate application for our time."[11]

Bible professor Michele Hershberger takes our understanding of biblical interpretation a step beyond salvation and ethics, writing, "The Bible needs to be read through a missional lens. God is and remains missional. The Bible is the story of God reaching out over and over again."[12] This becomes most clear in and though Jesus Christ.

## What is essential in Anabaptist Christianity?

Anabaptists have a high regard for the Scriptures and an even higher regard for Jesus. Jesus, even more than the Bible, is our final authority. Author Shane Claiborne says it clearly when he declares, "We believe in the infallible Word of God. His name is Jesus!"[13]

While Anabaptists affirm the inspiration and trustworthiness of Scripture, we are not strict literalists.[14] While the written words need to be taken seriously, all Scripture needs to be interpreted through the nature of Jesus, who is our Lord. It is important to interpret the Scriptures from a point of view that includes both the spirit and ethics of Jesus. We believe that the written Word and the spirit of Jesus must be held in creative tension. This is in contrast to many believers who interpret the Scriptures from a flat, dispensational, or spiritualized point of view.

Why would we say that Jesus, even more than the Bible, is our ultimate authority? The next chapter will help us to understand what it means to say "Jesus is Lord!"

## Questions for reflection and discussion

1. Which approach (flat Bible, dispensational, spiritualized Christ-centered, or ethical Christ-centered) have you used to interpret the Bible?

2. What disagreements between members of your family or church can you identify that are because of differing approaches to interpretation?

3. Reflect on the following contrasts within the Christian faith in regard to interpretation of Scripture:

| Many Christians emphasize: | Anabaptist Christians emphasize: |
|---|---|
| The Bible, rather than Jesus, as our final authority. | Jesus, rather than the Bible, as our final authority. |
| All Scriptures are inspired and equal in authority. | All Scriptures are inspired but not equal in authority. |
| The Old Testament reveals God's will for social ethics, while the New Testament is a guide for personal ethics. | Jesus, the fullest revelation of God and God's will, is the standard for both personal and social ethics. |
| Applications do not always need to coincide with the teachings and spirit of Jesus. | Applications must not counter the teachings and spirit of Jesus. |

4. What does it mean that the written Word and the spirit of Jesus must be held in tension? Can you give an example?

5. How should we reconcile the differences between what Moses says about adultery in Deuteronomy 22:22 and what Jesus says in John 8:1-11?

# THREE

# Jesus Is Lord

*God also highly exalted him and gave him the name that is
above every name, so that at the name of Jesus every knee
should bend, in heaven and on earth and under the earth,
and every tongue should confess that Jesus Christ is Lord, to
the glory of God the Father.*

*Philippians 2:9-11*

**E**ARLY CHRISTIANS grew in their understanding of Jesus. At first, they saw him as a rabbi or teacher. They noted that he was a teacher with unusual authority. For example, when Jesus delivered the Sermon on the Mount, "the crowds were astounded at his teaching, for he taught them as one having authority, and not as their scribes" (Matthew 7:28-29). When he died on the cross, the centurion and those who were with him exclaimed, "Truly this man was God's Son!" (Matthew 27:54).

On teaching tours, the disciples observed Jesus had authority to forgive sins, cast out demons, calm a stormy sea, and confront the money changers in the temple (Mark 2:10; 3:15; 4:39; 11:15-16). At the end of his ministry, Jesus said, "All authority in heaven and on earth has been given to me," and with that authority he commissioned his followers to "make disciples of all nations" (Matthew 28:18-19).

People were drawn to Jesus because he had authority and also because he related to them as a servant for their good. While secular people recognized Caesar as lord and were asked to show him their ultimate loyalty, the apostles, at the risk of their lives, dared to say, "Jesus is Lord!" He was their servant leader.

## How is lordship understood?

In a key instruction, Jesus said, "You know that the rulers of the Gentiles lord it over them, and their great ones are tyrants over them. It will not be so among you; but whoever wishes to be great among you must be your servant, and whoever wishes to be first among you must be your slave; just as the Son of Man came not to be served but to serve, and to give his life a ransom for many" (Matthew 20:25-28).

During the following centuries, however, leaders of the church did not follow Jesus' counsel. They began to "lord it over" each other and others just as secular leaders had done. The hierarchy of the church became increasingly dominant to the point that people, in effect, said, "The Pope is Lord."

Martin Luther rejected the authoritarian leadership of the Holy Roman Empire, and in its place developed a two-kingdom theology. This theology suggests that believers, in their personal lives, are called to be loyal to Jesus as Lord, but in their public lives, they are to be loyal to secular authorities, who have been ordained by God.

Anabaptists took another view. They believed that at all times and in all places, followers of Jesus are to give their supreme allegiance to God as known in Jesus Christ. They are to be *always* personally responsible for their actions. Followers of Christ are first of all citizens of God's kingdom, to which they owe ultimate allegiance. They are also citizens of a secular government, to which they are to give respect but not necessarily total obedience. Jesus instructed his followers to "strive first for the kingdom of God and his righteousness" (Matthew 6:33). When we fail to give Jesus and his kingdom our ultimate allegiance, we need to ask for forgiveness.

Jesus becomes Lord when we commit ourselves to following him in daily life. Because of his example and the coming of the Holy Spirit, we are enabled to think, feel, and act as he does. The apostle Peter wrote, "For to this you have been called, because Christ also suffered for you, leaving you an example, so that you should follow in his steps" (1 Peter 2:21). Following in Christ's steps is the goal of every Christian.

## Is Jesus both Savior and Lord?

Many believers who claim to be followers of Jesus are often quite incomplete in their surrender. Some who say "I have accepted Jesus as my Savior" continue to live their lives pretty much as they had before, less the sins they confessed. Even after baptism or confirmation, someone or something else is still in control of how they live their lives. Their acceptance of Jesus as Savior generally means they have asked God to forgive them for the bad habits, practices, and sins in which they have been involved. They say "Jesus is my Savior"—with lordship tacked on.

Instead of saying, "Jesus is my Savior and Lord," it might be better to give first place to lordship by saying, "Jesus is my *Lord* and Savior." From an Anabaptist perspective, lordship is the key issue and needs to be given priority. The primary sin from which we need forgiveness and deliverance is the sin of following other lords. It is these other lords and our allegiance to them that have caused us to sin. The first of the Ten Commandments says, "You shall have no other gods before me" (Exodus 20:3). The greatest offense of the Israelites was that they did not give their greatest, or ultimate, allegiance to God. They worshiped idols and followed the gods of the people around them. We have the same tendencies today.

## Who has ultimate authority over our lives?

One might say that in our world there are three forces seeking to claim ultimate authority. These are allegiance to self, secular leaders, and God as known through Jesus Christ. We will examine them beginning from the bottom of the illustration.

**Forces seeking ultimate authority**

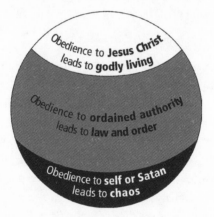

*The self as ultimate authority.*

Individuals and institutions are created good and for good purposes, but they tend to become selfish and therefore "fallen." In their fallen state, they seek selfishly to dominate and control rather than to serve.

The Genesis story tells us that Adam and Eve were tempted by Satan to believe that they could become like God and to independently know the difference between good and evil. That was not true. Jesus describes Satan as the "father of lies" (John 8:44). Satan's basic lie is that life is at its best when each person and organization is free to do as they please. The truth is, this kind of living leads to despair, chaos, and death.

Satan has sometimes been branded as a bully who simply goes about willfully destroying lives, marriages, and institutions. Might it be that Satan honestly believes that life is at its best when each of us is free to do as we please without regard to a higher authority? It is this selfish philosophy that destroys lives, marriages, and institutions.

Self-centered human beings and institutions join to form dominating systems. "These self-serving dominating systems," writes theologian Walter Wink in *The Powers That Be*, "lead to unjust economic relations, oppressive political relations, biased race relations, patriarchal gender relations, hierarchical power relations, and the use of violence to maintain them all."[1] The apostle Paul refers to these kinds of systems when he writes, "For our struggle is not against flesh and blood, but against the rulers, against the authorities, against the powers of this dark world and against the spiritual forces of evil in the heavenly realms" (Ephesians 6:12 NIV). It is encouraging to know that when believers are filled with the spirit of Jesus, living in community, and engaged in Christlike living, they are able to successfully battle against principalities and powers and to live a new life.

### Ordained leaders as ultimate authority.

God's first and greatest desire is that all people will follow his leadership and live according to his moral laws and principles. We are to seek first his kingdom; however, that is not what naturally or usually happens. People and organizations tend to live according to their own needs and desires. For this reason God has ordained secular leaders to guide and control those who do not place themselves under God's control. These secular authorities are ordained to create law and order in a fallen world.

People need to obey the highest laws and authority that they know. If they don't, the result will be chaos. The highest authority for most people is often a family member, employer, community or religious leader, military general, prime minister, or president. Anabaptist-minded Christians encourage each other to obey these leaders to the extent that Christian discipleship permits.[2] Obedience to ordained leaders leads to a society of order and law.

The Scriptures command us to be subject to the governing authorities that God has put in place. They have influence over us and are meant for our good. (See Romans 13:1-7.)

But while leaders and organizations are meant for our good, they all too often are fallen. Like individuals, they fall because they become selfish and misuse their power. They use it for their own selfish purposes or to lead us in a direction that is not helpful. When people follow self-seeking, dictatorial, or corrupt leaders, major problems and chaos are often the result.

### Jesus Christ as ultimate authority.

It is the conviction of Anabaptist-minded Christians that they can do more to bring law, order, and peace to this world if they obey their highest authority, who is Jesus Christ, than if they obey lower authorities. This is because the power of love goes beyond human laws. By following Jesus in daily life, the qualities and relationships of God's kingdom can become reality "on earth as it is in heaven" (Matthew 6:10).

When we allow God to lead us through Jesus, we will become persons who are influenced and who are influencing others to think, feel, and act in loving ways as Jesus did. The apostle Peter reminds us that "because Christ also suffered for you, leaving you an example . . . you should follow in his steps"

(1 Peter 2:21). Following in Christ's steps is the goal and objective of all Christians. It was and is especially important to Anabaptist-minded Christians.

## Who should receive supreme allegiance?

Most Christians still live with the tension inherent in Luther's theology. Under his two-kingdom theology, earthly, coercive government holds highest authority over how we are to live and act. As a result, Christians continue to obey government commands even if they conflict with the nature and spirit of Jesus. They obey Jesus in personal life but obey other authorities in public. For example, under normal circumstances, a Christian will never take the life of another human being. However, if serving in the army during a time of war and a military commander orders it, a Christian will take the life of another human being. In Luther's two-kingdom theology, it is assumed that the *government*, not the *person*, will be held accountable for taking the life of that other person.

Anabaptists disagree. We need to obey ordained leaders to the extent that Christian discipleship permits.[3] There will be times when faithful followers of Christ need to disobey commands that go contrary to their ultimate Lord. The apostle Paul encourages followers of Christ to be subject to secular authorities. Being subject does not mean blind obedience. To "be subject to" (Romans 13:1) secular authorities means to anticipate and respectfully submit to the punishment that leaders may place upon us for disobeying one of their commands or laws. When there is a conflict between the supreme ways of Jesus and the ordinary ways of secular leaders, Christians need to say with the early disciples, "We must obey God rather than any human authority" (Acts 5:29).

When I was pastor of a Mennonite church in Minnesota, I experienced the tension between obedience to Jesus and obedience to the secular government. A number of our members had served in the military. They had given their allegiance to the government and were willing to sacrifice their lives for their country. There were also many who, as conscientious objectors to war, had served their country in alternate ways. While both groups were willing to die for their country, the second group was not willing to kill for their country.

As would be expected, there was some conflict between the two groups. On Independence Day, the Fourth of July, which fell on a Sunday, the members of the church were surprised when I asked them to stand and pledge their allegiance to the flag of the United States. Then I asked them to turn 180 degrees and pledge their *supreme* allegiance to Jesus Christ. On a large screen were the words "We pledge our *supreme allegiance* to Jesus Christ and to the kingdom for which he stands; an eternal kingdom that offers love, justice, and hope for all."

The two groups in the congregation were united in recognizing that while they owed ordinary allegiance and respect to their national government, they owed their supreme allegiance to Jesus Christ.

## What is essential to Anabaptist Christianity?

While most Christians place greatest emphasis on Jesus as their Savior, Anabaptist believers seek to give equal or even higher emphasis to the lordship of Jesus. Saying "Jesus is Lord" is as important as saying "Jesus is my Savior." Jesus is to be the standard for both personal and social ethics. "Jesus is Lord" is a short but essential creedal statement of the Christian faith.

While the Scriptures are our ultimate source of information about God and God's will, we interpret the Scriptures through the spirit and nature of Jesus. In so doing, Jesus becomes our ultimate authority. As a result, Christians can do more to bring law, order, and peace to this world by following Jesus than by following lower levels of authority.

As followers of Jesus, we live with the tension of being citizens both of the kingdom of God led by Jesus and of a secular country led by elected and ordained officials. Regrettably, many Christians—including many current Anabaptists—are more obedient to their earthly leaders than they are to Jesus Christ. Followers of Christ need to say, day after day and week after week, that Jesus is Lord, and to follow that affirmation with appropriate and joyful actions.

Individuals need help and support to live under the lordship of Christ. That help and support comes through commitment to each other in community. The next three chapters explore the second core value: Community is the center of our life.

## Questions for reflection and discussion

1. Who or what authorities are seeking to rule over you and your life?

2. Reflect on the following contrasts that are emphasized within the Christian faith.

| Many Christians emphasize: | Anabaptists Christians emphasize: |
|---|---|
| Accepting Jesus as Lord and Savior | Accepting Jesus as Lord and Savior |
| Obeying government leaders even if their demands are contrary to the teaching and spirit of Jesus | Disobeying secular demands that are contrary to the teaching and spirit of Jesus |
| Shunning disloyalty to government at all costs | Being prepared to suffer for being supremely loyal to Jesus |
| Seeing government, rather than an individual soldier, as morally responsible for the killing and destruction that happens in war | Being personally and morally responsible for their actions; obedience to Christ is always the best way to live |

3. What does it mean that we obey authority "as far as discipleship will allow"? What will discipleship *not* allow?

4. What is the difference between saying "Jesus is my Savior and Lord" and saying "Jesus is my Lord and Savior"?

**Part II**

# Community
## Is the Center of Our Life

# FOUR

# Forgiveness Is Essential for Community

*Be kind to one another, tenderhearted, forgiving one*
*another, as God in Christ has forgiven you.*
Ephesians 4:32

**THE SECOND** core value of the Christian faith from an Anabaptist perspective is "Community is the center of our life." Professor, pastor, and college president Roberta Hestenes observes, "True community begins with God. Our God, who lives in community as Father, Son, and Holy Spirit, wants us to also experience the joys of close community!"[1]

In these next three chapters, I explore the concept of Christian community and what is needed for it to happen. This chapter focuses on vertical forgiveness (from God) needed for salvation and, more specifically, on horizontal forgiveness (from others) needed for community. Chapter 5 explores the giving and receiving of counsel, and chapter 6 describes how the church might be organized so that members experience a maximum sense of community.

## What is vertical forgiveness?

Vertical forgiveness is forgiveness from God. It can be depicted as the up-and-down beam of the cross. From the beginning of time, humans have felt the need to receive God's forgiveness. Adam and Eve needed forgiveness for their disobedience in the garden of Eden. Their oldest son, Cain, needed forgiveness when he murdered his brother, Abel. The children of Israel needed forgiveness for their disloyalty and idolatry. King David, after committing adultery, cried out, "Have mercy on me, O God . . . blot out my transgressions . . . and cleanse me from my sin" (Psalm 51:1-2).

**Vertical forgiveness**

Whenever humans disobey God, repentance and vertical forgiveness are needed. Vertical forgiveness is God's way of helping us overcome the alienation, guilt, fear, and shame caused by sin. It is a gift that restores fellowship with God, proper self-esteem, and confidence in the future.

As we review church history, we find four systems, or understandings, have been used to assure believers of their forgiveness from God. They are presented in the illustration.

**Four understandings of forgiveness**

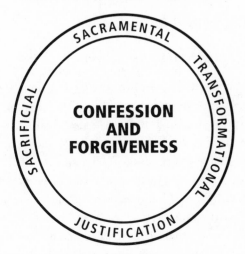

## The sacrificial understanding of forgiveness

This first understanding of forgiveness is based on the Old Testament sacrificial system. Sacrifices were a way for the people to deal with their guilt and shame for wrongdoing and the resultant alienation from God. The laws that God gave to the Israelites through Moses required sacrifices as payment for sins. People were to kill or send into the desert a sheep or a bull as a symbolic way of dealing with offensive thoughts and actions (see Leviticus 1–17).

The sacrificial understanding holds that the Old Testament sacrifices foreshadow the one perfect sacrifice of Jesus for the sin of the world. It sees Jesus as the Passover Lamb who, because of his great worth, was able to pay the penalty for all the sin of the world (see 1 Corinthians 5:7 and Hebrews 9:13–10:10).

While most Anabaptist Christians have accepted this understanding of how sins are paid for by a holy God, they also raise questions as to why a loving God would require an only Son to die a terrible death in order to bring about reconciliation. We are open to multiple understandings of forgiveness and atonement.

## The sacramental understanding of forgiveness

The sacramental system of forgiveness came into being through Augustine and the medieval church. People came to believe they could find forgiveness from God through religious rites or rituals known as *sacraments*. Over time, seven sacraments were adopted: baptism, confirmation, the eucharist, penance, ordination, marriage, and extreme unction. It was believed that these were given to the church as signs of God's grace. Actual confession or remorse for sin was sometimes rather shallow. Many came to believe that these practices in themselves brought relief and salvation to their lives.

Because of belief in original sin, the medieval church began baptizing infants as a means of removing that inherited sin. Because of the persistence of sins, the eucharist, representing the sacrifice of Christ, was repeatedly celebrated, just as the Old Testament sacrifices were repeated again and again. Extreme unction was offered for those nearing death, and prayers were said to Mary and the saints so that those in purgatory might be forgiven of remaining sin and be allowed to enter heaven more quickly.

Many Christians today continue to believe that the sacraments are either a means for receiving or a symbol of God's offer of forgiveness of sin. While Anabaptists respect those who hold to the sacramental understanding of forgiveness, it is not one that Anabaptists own.

## The justification by faith understanding of forgiveness

Justification by faith is largely based on Paul's words to the Ephesians, "For by grace you have been saved through faith, and this is not your own doing; it is the gift of God—not the result of works, so that no one may boast" (Ephesians 2:8-9). As a monk, Martin Luther had sought personal forgiveness by praying extensively, performing acts of penance, and practicing the sacraments, but all to no avail. He came to the conclusion that forgiveness and salvation did not come through such works. All a person needed to do to be justified before God was to have faith in the grace of God. Salvation from sin was God's work. It came by faith alone, not by anything a person might do.

The apostle Paul gave encouragement to this view by quoting Habakkuk 2:4: "The righteous will live by faith" (Romans 1:17 NIV). The doctrine of "justification by faith" separated Protestants from Catholics during the Reformation.

The justification by faith system teaches that when people have faith in what Jesus did on the cross, their sins will be forgiven and they will be made just before God. When someone places his or her faith in Christ's sacrificial death, God graciously declares that person to be "just" and able to go free, even though serious repentance and change of heart may be minimal.

Justification is a legal term in which a person who is technically guilty of committing a crime is deemed innocent by the court because of extenuating circumstances. For instance, a court may deem a person justified for breaking the speed limit if that person was driving too fast in order to get an expectant mother to the hospital. Those who adhere to this understanding of forgiveness believe that the sacrificial death of Jesus Christ is the extenuating or unusual circumstance that justifies the sinner before God. Christ's death on the cross is viewed as having paid the penalty of the person's sin. The individual is thus *justified* and allowed into the presence of God.

Some describe this view of forgiveness and salvation by saying that if a repentant person has faith in what God did in Christ, the blood of Christ will cover or wipe out that person's record of sin and replace it with Christ's righteousness. It is as if God sees this person as being sinless. (See 1 John 1:9.)

In this understanding, a person's nature does not change. By nature the person remains a sinner. It is expected that the person will continually sin and repeatedly need to plead for forgiveness. Right living or being obedient to Jesus in daily life is unrelated to God's evaluation of the person.

Our family saw an example of this in a friend who had been baptized as an infant and confirmed in his faith as a teenager. He became a leader in his youth group and regularly repeated words of confession and words of assurance of forgiveness during worship. But his faith seemed to make no difference in how he lived during the week. His testimony was "I'm not different; I'm just forgiven."

Anabaptists caution that relying on justification by faith alone can leave a person's life and actions largely unchanged. It places more emphasis on changing the attitude and actions of God toward us than on changing our attitudes and actions toward God and others. Dietrich Bonhoeffer called this "cheap grace." He wrote, "Cheap grace is the preaching of forgiveness without requiring repentance, baptism without obedience, Communion without confession, absolution without discipleship, and grace without the cross."[2]

## The transformational understanding of forgiveness

Early Anabaptists did not place their faith in sacrifices or sacraments, nor did they talk about justification by faith. As they pondered the life, teachings, death, and resurrection of Jesus, they came to understand that forgiveness and salvation come through honest repentance and a new openness to Jesus Christ. They believed and experienced that a person's nature can be changed from being a sinner who continually sins to being a saint empowered by the Holy Spirit to live a new, transformed life. Admittedly, the person still sometimes sins, but sinning is contrary to that person's new nature.

Early Anabaptists took much interest in what Jesus told Nicodemus: "No one can see the kingdom of God without being born from above" (John 3:3). They saw confession, forgiveness, and joyful obedience as means for being transformed by God from one nature into another. As with metamorphism in nature, a transformed life indicates that a person's nature has been changed.

"New birth" meant a new beginning. The early Anabaptists believed that life begins anew when a person turns from old loyalties, opens his or her life to the Holy Spirit, and begins living in obedience to Jesus Christ. The apostle Paul says that when a person enters into a relationship with Christ, "everything old" (thoughts, attitudes, actions, and relationships) "has passed away" and everything (thoughts, attitudes, actions, and relationships) "has become new" (2 Corinthians 5:17). This applies to both individuals and the church.

All views of salvation include confession and forgiveness. Anabaptist Christians emphasize the transformation that happens via confession, forgiveness, and new relationships. They believe that a healthy vertical relationship with God results in a transformed life that yields fruit. Such a life is best achieved through both honest repentance from sin and an obedient, Spirit-filled following of Jesus in daily life.

## What is horizontal forgiveness?

Horizontal forgiveness might be depicted as the sideways beam of the cross.

**Horizontal forgiveness**

While vertical forgiveness between a person and God is essential for salvation, Jesus actually had more to say about horizontal forgiveness—that is, the forgiveness that occurs between humans. For example, Jesus told his followers, "When you are offering your gift at the altar, if you remember that your brother or sister has something against you, leave your gift there before the altar and go; first be reconciled to your brother or sister, and then come and offer your gift" (Matthew 5:23-24). He also said, "If you forgive others their trespasses, your heavenly Father will forgive you; but if you do not forgive others, neither will your Father forgive your trespasses" (Matthew 6:14-15).

While most Christians have emphasized confessing their sins to God and receiving vertical divine forgiveness, early Anabaptist believers also placed great emphasis on the importance of confessing their offenses to each other and receiving horizontal human forgiveness.

Early Anabaptist believers often quoted Romans 12:2: "Do not be conformed to this world, but be transformed by the renewing of your minds." They expected all members—especially their leaders—to live saintly lives. They saw the church as being composed of people who kept their lives clean. When they detected sin and disobedience, it was to be confessed and dealt with. They would have agreed with Martin Luther King Jr., who said, "Forgiveness is not an occasional act. It is a consistent attitude."[3]

## How is horizontal forgiveness achieved?

Just as vertical forgiveness between God and an individual requires confession or repentance, so horizontal forgiveness requires confession or repentance. We come to right relationships with God and with each other through confession and forgiveness.

For true forgiveness to happen, a person must admit that what he or she said, felt, or did toward another person was wrong. The confessing person needs to approach the individual she or he offended and ask for forgiveness. This interaction usually represents the turning point in mending a broken relationship. It brings peace and closure to a conflict and helps the persons involved to think more clearly and act more warmly. Such confession and new life is essential for the existence of healthy community. It allows the participants to let go of negative emotions and desires. Forgiveness is needed for true community.

The gospel that Jesus proclaimed—and to which he encouraged his followers to give priority—was the good news of the kingdom's arrival (see Mark 1:14; Luke 9:2). The kingdom is where there are forgiven relationships with God and with each other. Human relationships are not possible without close communication. The deep desire of Jesus was that his followers would "be one, as we are one" (John 17:22).

The need for horizontal confession and forgiveness became evident when I came to my first pastorate. I soon discovered that Vernon, the chair of the congregation, and John, the chair of the elders (not their real names), were not on speaking terms. At a congregational meeting, Vernon had offended John by calling a suggestion that John made "stupid." While both Vernon and John had vertical relationships with God, they did not now have a horizontal relationship with each other. The tensions and their avoidance of each other began to affect the entire congregation.

Jesus' advice for such situations is, "If another member of the church sins against you, go and point out the fault when the two of you are alone" (Matthew 18:15). However, Vernon and John were either too shy or too stubborn to do this.

John, the elder, shared with me how pained and embarrassed he had been when Vernon made the cutting remark about his suggestion. When I talked with Vernon, he denied that he had meant any harm. A breakthrough came by bringing Vernon and John together, as Jesus instructed, to talk with each other face-to-face. In the meeting, I encouraged John to honestly share his pain and Vernon to carefully listen. As John shared, Vernon began to realize the reality of the harm he had caused. In a repentant spirit, he looked John in the eye and said, "John, I realize that I hurt you not only by what I said but also by how I said it. Will you forgive me?" After a painful pause, John reached out his hand and said, "I forgive you." The next Sunday, the two men were seen talking with each other in the vestibule. That act of horizontal forgiveness restored a sense of community not only to Vernon and John but also to the whole congregation.

"From Scripture and from our own experience, we know that relationships are important," observes April Yamasaki, lead pastor of Emmanuel Mennonite Church in Abbotsford, British Columbia. "Everywhere I look there are so many broken relationships.... Relationships can be hard work.... That's why church is important—not as a religious institution or something to go to every Sunday; not because it's perfect, because it's not; not because you won't ever get hurt, because you quite likely will. Real churches have real problems and blind spots, and wherever there are people there is also brokenness. But real church also means real relationship, with God and with others."[4]

## What takes place in horizontal forgiveness?

There are several kinds of forgiveness. *Transactional forgiveness* is when an offender confesses a fault and receives forgiveness from the offended. It is called transactional forgiveness because a *transaction* has taken place between the offender and the offended. Forgiveness of an offender releases that person from what he or she should be required to pay, and from the guilt and shame related to it.

Ken Sande, in his book *The Peacemaker*, writes, "True forgiveness will silently or otherwise communicate the following four promises:

- "I promise not to continue thinking about this incident."

- "I promise not to use this offense against you."

- "I promise not to talk to others about this incident."

- "I promise not to allow this incident to hinder our personal relationship."[5]

*Positional forgiveness* is when an offender refuses to confess what he or she has said, felt, or done. When there is no confession, a transaction is not possible. However, in positional forgiveness, the offended still holds an attitude or a position of forgiveness toward the offender.

Jesus practiced this kind of forgiveness when on the cross he prayed, "Father, forgive them; for they do not know what they are doing" (Luke 23:34). He was ready to forgive those who were sinning against him, even though they had not yet confessed their wrongdoing.[6] Counseling professor David Augsburger calls this kind of forgiveness *forgrieving*. It is called forgrieving because the offended *grieves* that, despite his or her openness to forgive, a transaction has not been completed and the relationship has not been restored.[7]

Positional forgiveness is for the benefit of the offended person. It helps an offended person to overcome inner anger and hurt that may lead to further emotional problems. An example of this became obvious on October 2, 2006, when Charles Carl Roberts entered an Amish one-room schoolhouse in the community of Nickel Mines, Pennsylvania, and shot ten young girls, killing five of them, before committing suicide in the schoolhouse. The Amish community held a forgiving attitude toward the shooter and his family. This unusual response was widely discussed in the national media. It was observed by many that the Amish don't expect life to be fair. They hold a forgiving position toward the world. When things go wrong, they are already in a forgiving mode, so the problem doesn't have a chance of growing into a story of resentment.[8]

The owners of a small Amish store offer a further example of positional forgiveness. They have posted a sign on a shelf of breakables: "If you break it, tell us so that we can forgive you."[9]

### What is the meaning of the cross?

The cross is a universal symbol of forgiveness. For early Christians, the cross symbolized Christ's sacrifice to pay for the sins of the world, but it also symbolized more than that. It symbolized the way Christ lived and the cost of living that way. Jesus instructed his followers to "take up their cross and follow me. For those who want to save their life will lose it, and those who lose their life for my sake will find it" (Matthew 16:24-25).

**The cross as symbol**

When most Christians take communion, they focus on their vertical forgiveness from God and on how the death of Christ paid for their sins. Communion becomes a rather somber experience. Although Anabaptist Christians observe communion as a remembrance of Christ's death, many also see communion as a fellowship meal in which they celebrate that they have been forgiven not only by God but also by those participating with them in communion. Instead of only remembering the heaviness of Christ's death, there is a joyful celebration because of the forgiven fellowship that exists.

## What is essential to Anabaptist Christianity?

Believers with an Anabaptist perspective recognize that vertical forgiveness from God is essential for salvation and that horizontal forgiveness from each other is essential for community. While Christians throughout history have emphasized vertical forgiveness from God, a vital balance between vertical and horizontal forgiveness is needed so that followers of Christ can have healthy, open relationships both with God and with each other. Healthy relationships are what the kingdom of God and the Christian faith are all about!

What else is needed for healthy community? In the next chapter we explore how we discern God's will by giving and receiving counsel in the body of Christ.

## Questions for reflection and discussion

1. Which of the four understandings of vertical forgiveness—sacrificial, sacramental, justification by faith, or transformational—have been primary in your experience?

2. How important to you is having strong horizontal relationships in your family and congregation? How might they be made stronger?

3. Reflect on the following contrasts that are experienced within the Christian faith.

| Many Christians emphasize: | Anabaptist Christians emphasize: |
|---|---|
| Vertical forgiveness | Horizontal forgiveness |
| Forgiveness through sacrifices, sacraments, or both | Transformation through faith, confession, and joyful obedience |
| Justification by faith alone | Honest repentance |
| Confession of sins in worship | Confession after having sinned |

4. What broken relationship have you experienced? Why is it so hard to confess wrongdoing and ask for forgiveness?

5. Have you or your family needed a third party as a go-between to help you achieve honest confession and forgiveness?

# FIVE

# God's Will Is Discerned in Community

*Be transformed by the renewing of your minds,*
*so that you may discern what is the will of God.*

Romans 12:2

**A** **UNIVERSAL CHALLENGE** for believers is how to know the will of God. It is always best to do God's will, but how do we discern it? In this chapter, we explore how the early Christians interacted in community to discern God's will, and then examine how some Anabaptist Christians today seek to determine God's will through giving and receiving counsel, especially in the context of preaching, teaching, and dialogue.

## How did early Christians discern God's will?

Jesus made it clear that his kingdom was not to be dictatorial in style. The Gospels are filled with illustrations of how Jesus and his followers asked each other questions such as "Which of these . . . was a neighbor?" (Luke 10:36); "What must I do to inherit eternal life?" (Luke 10:25); and "Who do people say I am?" (Mark 8:27). Each of these questions offered an excellent opportunity for Jesus and the community of disciples to give and receive counsel.

Because of the very nature of the church, the people of God are called to be a group of discerning people. Acts 15 tells the story of how the early church gathered for the Jerusalem Conference. Through reports from the field and the giving and receiving of counsel, a decision was reached on how new Christians of Gentile backgrounds were to be treated.

But from Constantine onward, church leadership became dictatorial in style. Priests, bishops, cardinals, and popes made many rules to regulate life in the church. Offenders were treated with harsh discipline. This dictatorial system remained in effect until the Protestant Reformation of the sixteenth century, when Martin Luther separated himself from this top-down style. He believed people could know the will of God through private Bible study and preaching.

Early Anabaptists developed patterns in which they discerned God's will together in community. Even today when new believers desire to join an Anabaptist congregation, they are typically asked, "Are you willing to give and receive counsel?" This question is key, because it indicates how that person will function not only in church but also in other areas of life. By promising to give and receive counsel, members admit that they need each other to discern and do the will of God.

In the early Anabaptist years, much discernment happened as members met in home groups. For example, Menno Simons spent a number of years going from house church to house church discussing the basic principles of Anabaptist thinking.

Despite Christ's commands to not be like the Gentile rulers who "lord it over" their subjects, many Christians today choose churches in which an authoritarian pastor tells them what to think and do. This approach does not adequately respect the gifts, abilities, and insights of the members. It leaves common members uninvolved in study and discernment, which may lead to lack of interest in the Scriptures and to members' inability to help each other discern vital issues. There is also danger that authoritarian leaders, who lack accountability to a discerning group, will lead their members astray.

## What is the hermeneutical community?

At first, Martin Luther believed any Christian could discern the will of God simply by reading the Scriptures and allowing the Holy Spirit to guide. It is rumored that he once said, "Any shepherd boy behind the bush with the Holy Spirit can interpret the Scriptures better than the pope."

This laissez-faire approach allowed each person to search the Scriptures and come to a personal conclusion about its meaning and application. Luther soon discovered that, all too often, individuals (including pastors) who studied and interpreted Scriptures on their own came up with misleading and false understandings.

Early Anabaptist leaders had high respect for the Scriptures and carefully studied them both individually and collectively. Rather than rely on experts, they felt that Spirit-directed believers who studied together were best able to understand the meaning and application of a Scripture for a particular situation and context. Such a group has sometimes been called a *hermeneutical*, or interpreting, community.

Through communal discernment, people of faith come to corporate understandings of God's will for a particular situation. While scholars may interpret a Scripture in general terms, Anabaptists believe that Spirit-directed persons who are acquainted with each other's life and work can best understand and interpret a Scripture for their situation.

Early Anabaptists courageously encouraged freedom of religious thought and practice. Through interactive visits, letters, pamphlets, and councils, they gave and received counsel that helped them to live faithfully in times of persecution. Their emphasis on community helped individuals to avoid either becoming isolated in their thinking or dictatorial in their decision making. Of notable importance was the group consensus reached through presentations and dialogue at the Schleitheim conference of 1527.[1] By taking the Scriptures, Jesus, the Holy Spirit, and each other seriously, leaders were able to come to consensus on seven topics: baptism, discipline, the Lord's Supper, separation from the world, shepherds (that is, pastors), nonresistance, and the oath.

## How is God's will discerned through preaching?

History and experience tell us that to adequately discern God's will, a healthy church needs a balance of three forms of communication. If any of these three is absent, or if the giving and receiving of counsel is absent in them, there is a lack in the discerning process. These three forms of communication are *preaching, teaching,* and *dialogue.*

The primary purpose of preaching has been to inspire listeners and call them to commitment. It is usually done in monologue form, from one individual to many, as shown in the diagram.

**Discernment through preaching**

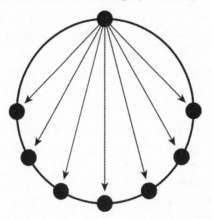

Jesus began his ministry by preaching. During his time on earth, he made many preaching tours throughout the regions of Galilee and Judea, inspiring large crowds and calling the people to commit themselves to the kingdom of God. Again and again, through preaching and storytelling, Jesus proclaimed qualities of the kingdom of God. It was in the context of kingdom relationships that God's will could be discerned.

The apostles continued the practice of preaching. Through a Jesus-centered message before a large crowd on the day of Pentecost, Peter inspired and called many to commitment. Three thousand people responded to his message that day! Later, the Holy Spirit "set apart" Paul and Barnabas to take the message of Christ to the Gentile world. (See Acts 2:41 and 13:2.) Paul went on to preach throughout the known world, inspiring both Jews and Gentiles with the message of Jesus and inviting them to follow a new master.

Preaching also characterized the early Anabaptists. Chosen members of the congregations did the preaching. Often there was a team, or "bench," of preachers who were prepared to preach anytime an opportunity presented itself. While preaching in that time was the domain of men, women were also active in sharing their faith. A third of the known martyrs were women.

Early Anabaptists preached with passion. For example, Hans Hut, an inspiring preacher, attracted large crowds and invited listeners to commitment. It is reported that he baptized more than five thousand new believers during his ministry. Others baptized even more.

While sometimes criticized, preaching is a necessary form of communication that helps people discern God's will. Unfortunately, when the teaching ministry of the church is weak, pastors tend to teach rather than preach. As a result, the pastor's sermons may lack inspiration and fail to call listeners to commitment. There is no substitute for solid biblical preaching that inspires and calls to commitment!

## How do pastors know what to preach?

The sermons of early Anabaptist pastors emerged from their personal study of the Scriptures and from their normal interactions with members of the church and community. This quite naturally would have included the giving and receiving of counsel and ideas.

How can this happen today? As pastor of Calvary Mennonite Church in Aurora, Oregon, I experienced a helpful discernment process that included the giving and receiving of counsel. On Monday and Tuesday mornings, I did private, exegetical study of the Scripture passage to be preached the following Sunday. On Wednesday mornings, three or four members of the congregation joined me in the church library to read the passage and over coffee discuss the meaning of the passage for our community. Through the give and take, I received many helpful insights as to how the message of the Scripture passage could be applied to the practical situations and needs in our church and community.

The Point Grey Inter-Mennonite Fellowship of Vancouver, British Columbia, has adopted a pattern that was common among earlier Anabaptists. Immediately after the message, the worship leader gives members the opportunity to comment, ask questions, or share further insights related to the main point of the sermon. This giving and receiving of counsel has caused those who preach to be more specific and those in the congregation to listen more carefully.

A number of thriving congregations use a pattern in which the preacher prepares a discussion outline based on the sermon to be used in small groups during the week. This encourages preachers to go beyond interpretation of the text and to become more oriented toward application. Members of the Meserete Kristos Church of Ethiopia believe this pattern is key to their rapid growth and reputation of being a "Bible teaching" church.

Some pastors lead a class, a group discussion, or a public forum after the worship service. Still others invite worshipers to come forward after the sermon for prayer or to receive ministry. All of these patterns provide opportunities for giving and receiving counsel in regard to the inspiration received or the commitments being made by the listeners.

## How is the will of God discerned through teaching?

While the primary purpose of preaching is to inspire and call to commitment, the primary purpose of teaching is to learn content. Teaching, as the diagram suggests, often happens in a question and answer format between the teacher and the students.

The Gospels lead us to believe that Jesus took three years to teach and train his disciples for their mission. He wanted his followers to thoroughly understand him and the nature of

God's kingdom. At the end of Jesus' ministry, he instructed his followers to "go . . . and make disciples of all nations . . . teaching them to obey everything that I have commanded you" (Matthew 28:19-20).

**Discernment through teaching**

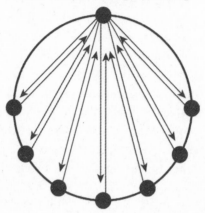

The early church continued the teaching and training process that Jesus had begun. Good information was needed to discern the will of God. It often took up to three years for new believers to be affirmed for membership.[2] Some believe that memorizing the Sermon on the Mount was part of the process.

Early Anabaptists also engaged in solid biblical study and teaching. In fact, the movement began in a Bible study group! Leaders learned the Scriptures well and arranged Scripture verses according to subject. Several prepared thematic concordances, which they shared with each other. Through these concordances, they gave and received counsel about the content, relationships, and meaning of the Scriptures.

## How is teaching done today?

The freedom to teach their children and youth has been important for Anabaptist Christians. This freedom has been so important that, when persecuted, Anabaptists have moved to locations where they had permission to conduct their own schools in their own way. Groups of families moved to Alsace in France, to the Vistula Valley of Poland, to Russia, and at multiple times to countries in North and South America.

For many years, the youth and adult Sunday school classes in Mennonite churches were the primary settings for the learning of content. The congregation of 130 members in which I grew up had a class for each age group in the church—sixteen in all! These became the settings or frames of reference for members to give and receive counsel.

In North America, Mennonites currently sponsor thirty primary and secondary schools, a dozen colleges, and at least three seminaries. These are primary locations for the giving and receiving of counsel in regard to Anabaptist faith and practice.

There is currently considerable anxiety in many Mennonite circles about biblical illiteracy. However, more and more options for study are emerging. These include seminars of various kinds, workshops at annual conferences, webinars launched by seminaries, and a variety of online courses from different sources.

## How is God's will discerned through dialogue?

While the primary purpose of preaching is to inspire listeners and call them to commitment, and the primary purpose of teaching is for participants to learn content, the primary purpose of dialogue is for members to *apply* what they have heard and learned to their lives and situations. As the diagram shows, dialogue is interactive communication between members in conversational style.

Jesus, the apostles, and the reformers all engaged in considerable dialogue. In the early church, this dialogue often took place in small group and home settings. Early Anabaptists also met face-to-face in small groups and house church settings. These intimate interactions were in contrast to the more formal preaching and teaching settings of mainline and state churches.

**Discernment through dialogue**

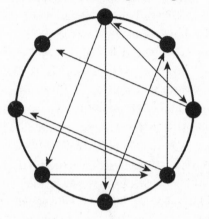

Something essential happened to early Anabaptists when they met in small groups. In the context of close community and intimate dialogue, they were able to experience the presence of Christ and follow through with obedient action.

## How does dialogue happen today?

Small groups offer an excellent setting for believers and seekers to give and receive counsel on what they have heard, learned, or experienced. Congregations that are experiencing renewal and growth inevitably have a strong emphasis on small groups. We'll look at small groups more closely in the next chapter.

Dialogue is essential for helping believers to be accountable. I have committed myself to not making any major decision without first discussing the matter with my accountability group. Through giving and receiving counsel, the group helps me to understand a problem, think of new options for solving it, and set goals for what is to be accomplished. Sometimes I am affirmed in my thinking, while at other times I am challenged to explore other options.

In its early days, Assembly Mennonite Church in Goshen, Indiana, developed a rigorous way of helping members discern God's will for their lives. During the first week of the new year, members of small groups asked each other, "How did you use your time during the past year, and how do you hope to use it in the coming year?" During the second week, the question for dialogue was, "How did you use your talents during the previous year, and how do you hope to use them in the year ahead?" During the third week the dialogue became even more personal. The question was, "How much money did you earn, and how do you hope to earn and spend money in the year ahead?" One member said, "It took considerable maturity for us to give and receive counsel at such vulnerable levels, but we found that such interaction was a strong key in enabling us to discern the will of God for our lives."[3]

Jessica Reesor Rempel and Chris Brnjas were both finishing their theology degrees when they began to notice that many young adult peers felt disconnected from church, even though their Anabaptist faith was important to them. They started Pastors in Exile, which aims to connect young people through dialogue and vibrant faith experiences inside and outside church walls. Reesor Rempel now facilitates a weekly intergenerational feminist Bible study where participants discern God's will for themselves and for each other through giving and receiving counsel. Although feminism would have been far from the minds of the sixteenth-century Anabaptists, Reesor Rempel and Brnjas note the resemblance of the experience. Reesor Rempel explains, "As we read [the Bible] we ask questions about power, privilege, gender roles, and the nature of God that we have not been encouraged to ask in a larger church setting. When we gather there are no authorities or experts;

rather, each participant is invited to explore her own interpretation of the Scripture with the group. Everyone has something to teach and everyone has something to learn."[4]

As director of the Hesston College pastoral ministries program, I found that dialogue was essential in helping individuals discern a call to ministry. Candidates needed to have both an inner call and an outer call to discern whether their call was from God. The inner call involved being in personal dialogue with God and self to discern passions, thoughts, and values. The outer call came when an outside individual or group discerned that the person had the gifts, personality, and passion for the task being considered. Regional conference pastor John Powell observes that "through congregational discernment, the congregation calls and gives authority to people to lead. This 'authority' differs in each congregation. Some leaders lead with tremendous latitude while others are restricted by formal and informal structures."[5]

## What is essential to Anabaptist Christianity?

Out of necessity and due to persecution, early Anabaptists were forced out of large congregational settings and into more intimate settings, where the giving and receiving of counsel was common. Today the giving and receiving of counsel is encouraged by asking members upon entrance into the community, "Are you willing to give and receive counsel?" This question helps members resist the tendency to be either laissez-faire or dictatorial.

From experience, we have learned that for good discernment to take place, congregations generally need a good balance of preaching, teaching, and dialogue.

What is the best setting for discernment and in-depth community to happen? In the next chapter, we examine the rich experiences that become possible in small groups.

## Questions for reflection and discussion

1. Does your church ask incoming members, "Are you willing to give and receive counsel in the context of this congregation?" Why or why not?

2. Reflect on the following ways that believers in the Christian faith discern God's will.

| Many Christians emphasize: | Anabaptists Christians emphasize: |
|---|---|
| Discerning God's will through private study and prayer. | Studying and interpreting the Scriptures in dialogue. |
| Preaching is most important. | A balance of preaching, teaching, and dialogue is important. |
| Telling people what they should think or do. | Helping members make decisions through giving and receiving counsel. |

3. In what situations have you asked for advice or counsel from others? Why do you need to ask for advice or counsel?

4. How have you been helped to discern God's will or call for your life? How was it intimidating? How was it helpful?

# SIX

# Members Are Held Accountable

*They broke bread at home and ate their food with glad
and generous hearts, praising God and having
the goodwill of all the people.*

*Acts 2:46-47*

**THE UNIQUENESS** of the Anabaptist faith is probably as much in its form as in its theology. After studying sixty-two doctoral dissertations on Anabaptist beginnings, pastor Takashi Yamada, a scholar from Japan, came to the conclusion that "the uniqueness of both the early church and the early Anabaptists was that they met in small groups where they confronted each other and made each other strong enough to confront the world."[1]

In this chapter we will explore small groups as a way of organizing the church for maximum community, effectiveness, and accountability. We will see how being part of a Spirit-filled small group may be the closest we will come to experiencing the kingdom of God on earth.

## What is the kingdom of God?

Jesus began his ministry by proclaiming that the kingdom of God had come near and that prophecies about it were being fulfilled (Mark 1:14; Luke 4:14-19). He soon selected a diverse group of twelve disciples for specific training, teaching them to pray "Your kingdom come. Your will be done, on earth as it is in heaven" (Matthew 6:10), and "sent them out to proclaim the kingdom of God" (Luke 9:2).

While on earth, Jesus repeatedly preached the gospel of the kingdom. His parables often illustrated qualities of the kingdom. The kingdom was so important to him that he spent his final forty days on earth "speaking about the kingdom of God" (Acts 1:3). While Paul preached the gospel of grace, he apparently also preached this same "kingdom of God" message everywhere he went (Acts 19:8; 20:25; 28:23, 31).

It might be said that the kingdom of God is present wherever God is king. This means being accountable to the king. If God is king of your life, "The kingdom of God is within you" (Luke 17:21 KJV). If God is king of your family or group, "The Kingdom of God is already among you" (Luke 17:21 NLT). Scripture would lead us to believe that the kingdom is both here and not yet. At the end of time when we are in the full presence of God, we will experience the kingdom of God in all its fullness (Revelation 21:7). A Spirit-filled small group brings qualities of the kingdom into the present.

God's kingdom is made of loving relationships, not political power. Jesus wants us to have the quality of relationship that he had and still has with his Father. While on earth, he prayed that his followers would be one in their fellowship, as he and the Father were one (John 17:22). To have that kind of fellowship, we are invited to repent of anything false and commit ourselves to loving the Lord our God with all our heart, soul, mind, and strength (see Mark 12:29-31).

Jesus was also accountable to his Father. He told his disciples, "I can do nothing on my own. . . . I seek to do not my own will but the will of him who sent me" (John 5:30). In the end we will all be held accountable for what we have done.

Followers of Constantine and Augustine taught that the church itself was the kingdom of God. While early Anabaptists aspired to be a perfect church, they recognized that while the church can proclaim the kingdom and be a foretaste of it, the church cannot be the kingdom of God.

The identity of early Anabaptist Christians was tied to their understanding of the kingdom. They saw a marked contrast between the kingdom of God and the kingdoms of this world. Their commitment to kingdom thinking and living moved them away from individualistic faith and complex ecclesiastical structures. It helped them to develop strong concepts of living in community where they were held accountable.

## How can the church be viewed?

The church has sometimes been depicted as a two-winged bird. One wing represents the larger, organized congregation, while the other wing represents its smaller, face-to-face groups. These two wings need to be in balance. The teaching program of the church may be seen as the tail that stabilizes the congregation.[2]

God has always used both large and small groups to accomplish his purposes. While Moses led a large group of former slaves into the wilderness, Jethro, his father-in-law, encouraged him to divide that large congregation into small groups. Jesus preached to large crowds numbering in the thousands but spent most of his time nurturing a small group of twelve.

**The two-winged church**

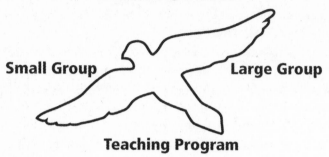

**Small Group**     **Large Group**

**Teaching Program**

According to Acts 2, the first Christians gathered in a large group in the temple courts to be taught by the apostles. They also met in small groups in each other's homes to eat, fellowship, pray, and have communion together. In addition, they were generous in sharing their resources with each other. It was in these small groups that they most held each other accountable to live as Jesus had lived.

We are told that these early church members not only had good relationships with each other but also had "the goodwill of all the people" in the community. As a result, "the Lord added to their number those who were being saved" (Acts 2:47). One of the reasons the early church grew so rapidly was the love and care they felt for one another. "Mutual support and accountability appear to have been central to the early Christian community's growth," notes theologian Reta Halteman Finger.[3]

But as time passed, energy that was once invested in ministry and relationships was channeled into defining doctrines, organizing church systems, and building church structures. The emphasis on meeting in small groups for fellowship, sharing, and accountability was largely lost. Instead of experiencing the presence of Christ in the context of small groups, believers were encouraged to experience the presence of Christ via the sacraments. Instead of being present for each other, they were encouraged to be present for the serving of the eucharist. Those who wanted to obediently follow Jesus and experience a close sense of community lived separately in monasteries and convents.

While Martin Luther and other mainline reformers may have hoped to reform the church to New Testament patterns, their associations with the government and higher classes of people caused them to continue in the context of large state-supported churches. Meanwhile, parallel to the early church experience, Anabaptist believers, because of persecution, met in small, face-to-face groups in homes and secret settings where they experienced close fellowship, forgiveness, and encouragement to follow Jesus in daily life. It appears that in many settings a small face-to-face relational group rather than a congregation was the basic unit of the church.

## What is a small group?

A small group can look different in different places and different settings. In most North American settings, small groups can be defined, according to Christian formation scholar Roberta Hestenes, as "an intentional face-to-face gathering of three to twelve people that meet on a regular time schedule for the purpose of support and spiritual growth."[4] When a group has more than twelve individuals, it is considered to be a large group. In a large group, members generally sit in rows. Their focus tends to be on a subject, agenda, or leader. In a small group, members usually sit in a circle where they can have eye contact with each other. The focus is generally on the individuals in the group, on their common concerns, and on what is happening in their lives.

Small groups are the basic unit of the church. They network to form congregations, congregations network to form denominations, and denominations network to constitute the church universal.

## What happens in a small group?

Small groups provide a space for meeting people's needs and for holding members accountable for meeting the needs of the others in the group. Small groups offer members a sense of belonging and a place for spiritual growth as well as settings for fun, fellowship, and interaction. In small groups, members are helped to discover their gifts, to be mobilized for service, and to offer mercy and compassion to each other as needed.

I believe that small groups are the best thing that has happened to the church since the Reformation. The Reformation returned the Bible to the people; small groups are returning ministry to the people. Basic needs are often best met in small groups of twelve or less. If the church is where we study the Scriptures, pray for each other, and are present for each other in time of need, this often happens best in the context of small groups.

People go to where their needs are met. They go to school when they need learning. They go to a doctor when they need medical help. They go home at the end of the day for food and rest. More and more people around the world are going to small groups to satisfy their needs for deeper relationships, a more meaningful spiritual life, and emotional support.

Early Anabaptist leaders were probably influenced as much or more by the monastic movement as by what was happening in the Protestant Reformation. While most believers continued to meet in cathedrals and parish churches, Anabaptists met in small groups where they developed close relationships and held each other accountable. "It is often in small circles of fellowship that we feel the most deeply understood by others and receive the strength we need to face the difficult times in life," says Ervin Stutzman, executive director of Mennonite Church USA.[5]

## How important are small groups in the church?

Most congregations in Canada and the United States are program-oriented. Such congregations often have small groups as one program of the church, as shown in the diagram.

**Program-based church**

In a program-based congregation, members give primary emphasis to the activities of the church. As one of its programs, small groups may need to compete with worship, a Sunday school program, and a mission project for time and priority.

The advantage of this type of church is that through its various programs it can provide a great variety of subjects, themes, and activities. The disadvantage is that members often find it difficult to go deeply into any one of the emphasized areas, and therefore little is achieved.

A second type of church is a congregation *of* small groups. Instead of being a congregation *with* groups as a program, it is a congregation consisting *of* groups. All members belong, first and foremost, to a small group, and then to a congregation. A small group–based church often concentrates on one theme at a time. Often an outline of the Sunday sermon is prepared for discussion and application in small groups. This pattern allows the congregation and its members to concentrate and go deeper one theme at a time.

### Small group–based church

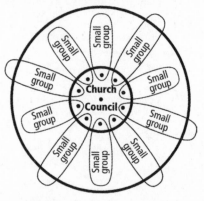

In a church *of* small groups, the small groups more readily become the key organizational and pastoral structure of the church. The group leaders often function as lay pastors to their members, even to the point of serving them communion. When someone is ill, troubled, or challenged, the small group leader or a group member is the first to respond. While the congregation's lead pastor remains available, the lead pastor is not expected to fulfill the routine needs of the members.

Assembly Mennonite Church of Goshen, Indiana, is a helpful example of a congregation *of* groups. Membership in the congregation is via a small group. Small groups provide opportunities for fellowship, study, mutual care, and outreach. When an issue arises, it is discussed within the groups, then referred to the council of elders. Or if the issue originates in the council, it is discussed in the groups and referred back. A member from each group constitutes the church's team of elders.

A church *of* small groups rather than merely *with* small groups may not need a fellowship committee, an adult Sunday school class, or an evangelism committee, because these functions are being fulfilled in the small groups. The groups may upon occasion take turns leading the congregation in worship, planning a seminar, or organizing an all-church retreat. Group leaders may serve as the congregation's board of elders.

The Meeting House of Oakville, Ontario, affiliated with the Brethren in Christ denomination, is a model of a contemporary Anabaptist small group–based church. The Meeting House has eighteen satellite congregations that meet simultaneously in various movie theaters and other venues located within fifty miles of its central campus. Each satellite congregation has its own pastor, but the preaching is done from the Oakville center, then discussed in small groups, called "home churches." While The Meeting House has a total membership of more than five thousand, a site pastor advised me, "If you want to truly experience the church, you must be part of one of our small groups. Small groups are where it happens!"

## What is causing growth in the Global South?

The story of the Meserete Kristos Church of Ethiopia is helping us to relearn what was essential to the early and Anabaptist churches. In 1982, the denomination was composed of fourteen congregations with approximately five thousand members. That year a repressive government imprisoned pastors and forced those fourteen congregations to close. In creative response to this problem, the elders prepared study guides and encouraged all members to meet weekly in home groups of seven or less. When a group grew to nine, the members were encouraged to form a new group. For eight years it was in these small groups where members were nurtured and held each other accountable to live their faith.

When the governmental restrictions were lifted, everyone was surprised to find that the church had grown from fourteen to fifty congregations, and from five thousand to more than fifty thousand members! Meserete Kristos Church has continued with its strong emphasis on small groups and has now grown to more than seven hundred congregations with more than four hundred thousand attendees!

According to sociologist Conrad Kanagy, churches in general and Anabaptist churches in particular are growing most rapidly in the Global South.[6] With coauthors Tilahun Beyene and Richard Showalter, Kanagy reports that in the past thirty-five years, Anabaptist believers have increased fourfold in Asia and Central America, and sevenfold in Africa.

Much of the vitality of these growing churches in the Global South is because of a strong emphasis on small groups. An Ethiopian pastor told me, "You can miss Sunday morning worship but you better not miss the Wednesday night meeting in the homes or you will lose your faith!"

Kanagy, Beyene, and Showalter write, "Anabaptism in the Global South has much in common with its sixteenth-century origins—perhaps more so than does contemporary Anabaptism in North America and Europe."[7]

## How often should a small group meet?

It is generally true that the more often a group meets together, the closer the members are drawn to Christ and to each other. Early church and early Anabaptist groups met weekly or even more frequently. Small groups that meet monthly, as is customary in program-based churches, have limited impact on their members. Influence on the thinking, relationships, and joyful obedience of members increases exponentially according to the frequency of their meetings.

The question of how often a small group should meet is related to how important a sense of community is to the individuals in the group. If programs and activities are most important, they will consume primary energy and time. However,

**Frequency and influence of small group meetings**

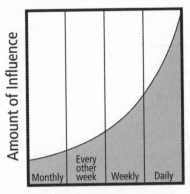

Frequency of meetings

if depth of fellowship, spiritual growth, and living rightly are most important, priority may be given to a weekly small group meeting instead of to programs. Congregations composed of groups often discover that the key gifts their church has to offer are fellowship and support for mission. They experience community and accountability in the context of small groups.

## What is essential to Anabaptist Christianity?

As in early Anabaptist times, in today's churches there is often a marked difference between program-based churches with small groups and congregations that are composed of small groups. Small group–based churches focus more clearly on the growth and well-being of their members and those they are seeking to reach. Small groups, sometimes called care groups, are often the best setting for meeting the needs of people and for helping them to meet the needs of others.

In the first core value, we affirmed that Jesus is the center of our faith. In this second part, we have affirmed that community is the center of our life. We move now to the third core value: Reconciliation is the center of our work.

## Questions for reflection and discussion

1. In what ways or places are you currently experiencing Christian community?

2. Reflect on the following contrasts between program-based churches *with* groups and small group–based churches that are composed *of* groups.

| A church *with* groups emphasizes: | A church *of* small groups emphasizes: |
|---|---|
| The church as an organization with various programs. | The church as a family composed of fellowship groups. |
| The worshiping congregation is the basic unit of the church. | The small group is the basic unit of the church. |
| A sanctuary is the basic meeting place for the congregation. | Homes, offices, and restaurants are often their meeting places. |
| The pastor is the primary source of pastoral care for the members. | Group leaders and members are the congregation's primary caregivers. |
| Members are held accountable for responsibilities in their programs. | Members are held accountable for their personal lives. |

3. If you are a member of a small group, which of the following needs are being met in your group?

   \_\_\_ A sense of belonging    \_\_\_ Welcoming new people

   \_\_\_ Spiritual growth           \_\_\_ Discovering your gifts

   \_\_\_ Fun and fellowship      \_\_\_ Being mobilized for service

   \_\_\_ Sharing and prayer      \_\_\_ Receiving mercy and compassion

4. Which of the following purposes would you like to be primary for your group?

   \_\_\_ To experience friendship and social relationships

   \_\_\_ To experience substantive sharing and prayer

   \_\_\_ To experience Bible study and spiritual growth

   \_\_\_ To receive support for mission and service

   \_\_\_ Other: _____

**Part III**

# Reconciliation
## Is the Center of Our Work

# SEVEN

# Individuals Are Reconciled to God

*If anyone is in Christ, there is a new creation: everything old has passed away; see, everything has become new! All this is from God, who reconciled us to himself through Christ, and has given us the ministry of reconciliation.*

*2 Corinthians 5:17-18*

WHILE SOME FOLLOWERS of Christ say evangelism is at the center of our work, others say peacebuilding is most important. In truth, both evangelism and peacebuilding are essential. Our third core value brings these two aspects of the Christian faith together in the word *reconciliation*.

Reconciliation has to do with restoring relationships. It is the bringing together of persons, ideas, or accounts that have been in conflict. Reconciliation assumes that at one time fellowship existed; however an offense took place that brought about estrangement and perhaps hostility, which needs to be resolved.

In this chapter, we explore how we are personally reconciled to God and how we seek to help others become reconciled to God. In chapter 8, we will explore how members are reconciled to each other in the church. Chapter 9 discusses how we seek to reconcile conflicted people in the world.

## What is needed for reconciliation?

Basic to Anabaptist faith is that each person needs to make an individual decision or series of decisions to accept God's offer of forgiveness and invitation to joyful obedience. Early Anabaptists did not think it was adequate, as did the prevailing church, to simply be a citizen of a jurisdiction that was called Christian. They believed that when it came to reconciliation with God, a clear decision needed to be made. They repeatedly quoted Jesus, who said, "Not everyone who says to me 'Lord, Lord,' will enter the kingdom of heaven, but only the one who does the will of my Father in heaven" (Matthew 7:21).

Making a specific decision was especially significant for first-generation Anabaptists. In later times, children, in the context of their believing homes, often accepted God's grace and followed the ways of Jesus. For both first-generation Anabaptists and their believing children, baptism announced their desire and decision to live according to God's grace and God's way.

As we consider individual reconciliation, it is not God who needs to be reconciled to us or to make a decision. God has not sinned or offended us, but rather has always longed for a loving relationship with each of us. It is we who have erred. We need to be relationally restored to God and God's will.

Inaccurate concepts of God are also cause for concern. God sent his Son, Jesus, to this earth to reconcile us to a misunderstood God. The world needed to know God as a loving, nurturing parent who is compassionate and full of mercy but who is also powerful and determined enough to make things come out in some fair way. Being in relationship with this God makes a difference. Philosopher Robert Solomon writes, "Our belief in this just and loving God and our commitment to join God's work leads us to conclude that justice will be served either in this life or the next."[1]

## What is salvation?

Mennonite historian C. Arnold Snyder says, "In my view the heart and soul of the Anabaptist movement is found in its understanding of salvation."[2] Anabaptists understand salvation in terms of reconciliation and transformation. To be *saved* means to be reconciled to God and God's family. As we are reconciled to God, as known in Christ and Christ's body, we are transformed in how we think, feel, and act.

Snyder observes that radical Anabaptist reformers believed that regeneration, or inner change of human nature, was possible. They believed that by the power of God, "sinners are reborn and regenerated by the Holy Spirit, and become new persons. These new persons then live lives that give witness to the sanctification that God's grace is working in their lives."[3]

Transformation is the goal. When we are willing and obedient, God changes us into what we are meant to be. When that change takes place, it is good news! It is good news not only for the individual but also for those to whom that individual relates. A true relationship with God results in works of love.[4]

Jim Wallis, editor of *Sojourners* magazine, describes the transformational, or saving, process by saying, "The New Testament stresses the necessity of a radical turnabout and invites us to pursue an entirely different course of life. Thus, conversion is far more than an emotional release and much more than an intellectual adherence to correct doctrine. It is a basic change in life direction."[5]

For early Anabaptists, following Jesus in daily life was not fundamentally an issue of obedience to the law but rather a result of God's grace and regeneration enabling it. "Law is not capable of changing the heart," said Pilgram Marpeck, an early Anabaptist. "Only God and God's gracious Spirit can do that."

Anabaptists viewed salvation differently from both Catholic and Protestant believers. Anabaptists did not believe in original sin and therefore did not believe that infant baptism or other sacraments were required to save a person from eternal punishment. Further, most Anabaptists took issue with predestination, which places all the responsibility for salvation on God. They insisted that while salvation is by the grace of God, individuals need to decide to accept or reject God's offer and invitation. Furthermore, Anabaptists did not believe that justification by faith was, by itself, an adequate understanding of salvation. They believed that there needed to be a transforming work of the Holy Spirit and a commitment to following Jesus in daily life.

## What kind of transformation takes place?

How might we understand the transforming work of the Holy Spirit? First, we must understand that transformation is God's work. None of us can overcome our shortcomings and live a Christlike life without God's help. Even if we could alter our outer actions by our own will, only God can change our hearts and inner spirit.

For the Anabaptists, salvation through Christ meant yielding to God and being remade into a new person empowered to live a different kind of life. There was a wholeness in the Anabaptist understanding of reconciliation.

When a person is relationally restored to God, that person is saved, or delivered, from the evil or conflict that was being experienced. That evil and conflict may have been in a variety of areas. Evangelist Myron Augsburger says, "The Mennonite evangel seeks to save a person as a whole being: body, soul, and spirit."[6] The late David Schroeder, a professor at Canadian Mennonite Bible College, said, "When we are saved, we should be able to specifically name that from which we have been delivered."[7]

God's work of transformation can be described in terms of creation, fall, and redemption, as shown in the diagrams that follow.[8]

## Created in God's image

Our God is a thinking, feeling, acting God who, in essence, is Spirit. This thinking God created the universe and all that is in it. This feeling God expresses both compassion and righteous anger. This acting God delivered the children of Israel from slavery and is continuing to deliver us from bondages of every kind.

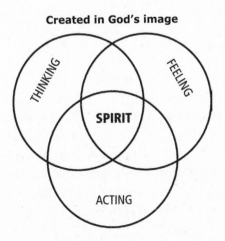

**Created in God's image**

THINKING  FEELING

SPIRIT

ACTING

Because we are created in God's image, we too are thinking, feeling, and acting individuals who are essentially spiritual in nature. Our real self is our inner spirit. It cannot be seen, but it determines who we are and for what we will be known. Our bodies are the visible structures through which our spirits are expressed. When God's Spirit is within us, we will be able to think, feel, and act in a way that represents God.

## Fallen because of sin

Unfortunately, all of us go astray and "fall short of the glory of God" (Romans 3:23). Instead of the Spirit of God being our center, we tend to place self at the core of our being. In a fallen, sinful state, we might be depicted as in the following diagram.

**The fallen state**

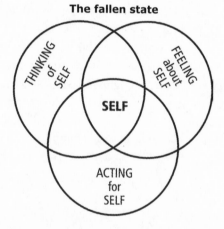

In the Mennonite Church USA "Purposeful Plan," the denomination's leaders write, "Because of sin, all have fallen short of the Creator's intent, marred the image of God in which we were created, disrupted order in the world, and limited our love for others. Therefore, through the reconciling power of Jesus Christ, we seek to walk in righteousness, or 'right-relatedness' with God and others."[9]

When self, instead of the Spirit of God, is at the center, we tend to pursue our own thoughts, be preoccupied with our own feelings, and act in regard to our own self-interests—even if those thoughts, feelings, and actions are not the best for those to whom we relate. The apostle Paul states, "Anyone who does not have the Spirit of Christ does not belong to him" (Romans 8:9). The wages, or result, of selfish living is the death of enthusiasm, relationships, and hope (see Romans 6:23).

Beliefs determine feelings, and feelings determine actions. The way we think affects the way we feel about things, and the way we feel influences the way we act. When the self is dominant, we become self-centered in our thoughts, attitudes, and actions. The apostle Paul says, "Those who live following their sinful selves think only about things that their sinful selves want" (Romans 8:5 NCV).

## Redeemed and transformed by Christ

Jesus began his ministry by calling us to "repent and believe in the good news" (Mark 1:15). To be transformed, we need to go through a time of repentance and turning from old thoughts, feelings, and actions. "It is through death—to our former practices, old habits and bad attitudes—that the Holy Spirit remodels our life," states pastor Darren Petker. "The Holy Spirit is continually making us new as we die to old behaviours and thought patterns, so that in their place new life can take root. Jesus knew full well that death was required for new life to begin. He willfully laid down his life so that the power of his resurrection could transform us."[10]

When we repent of our selfish thoughts, attitudes, and actions and open our lives to God's Spirit, we are transformed. A transformed person might be pictured as shown in the diagram.

**The transformed person**

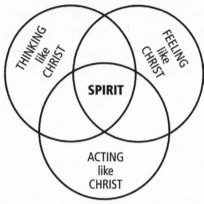

Early Anabaptist leaders spoke with enthusiasm about the transforming power of the Holy Spirit. They believed that the Holy Spirit made it possible for believers to follow Jesus in their daily lives. They were convinced that it was possible for them to be transformed into what God wanted them to be. They believed that it was possible to be "born again": given a new start with new core values, disciplines, and inner power. They believed that with a new inner spirit we are able to think, feel, and act like Christ!

## How will we be known?

When we have a new spirit at our center, we will attain a new identity. Our thoughts, feelings, and actions will convey a new reality. Instead of being preoccupied with self, we will have something to give. "Christianity is not a religion or a philosophy," says Rick Warren, pastor of Saddleback Community Church. "It is a relationship and lifestyle. The core of that lifestyle is thinking of others, as Jesus did, instead of ourselves. Thinking of others is the heart of Christlikeness and the best evidence of spiritual growth."[11]

## As student-teachers

In our *thinking*, we will become known as student-teachers. The apostle Paul writes, "Be transformed by the renewing of your minds" (Romans 12:2). He describes that transformed identity by saying, "Let the same mind be in you that was in Christ Jesus" (Philippians 2:5).

As we study the life, teachings, and ministry of Jesus, we begin thinking like Jesus, and then, as we relate to family, friends, and neighbors, we begin to teach what we have learned. In other words, we become student-teachers! We are students who learn from Jesus, and simultaneously we are teachers who pass on to others what we have learned!

## As forgiven reconcilers

In our *feelings*, we will become known as forgiven reconcilers. "Be . . . tenderhearted, forgiving one another, as God in Christ has forgiven you" encourages the apostle Paul (Ephesians 4:32). As we become transformed, we shed former emotions and begin to develop attitudes toward others that God has had toward us. The Holy Spirit gives us the ability to convey to others the "love, joy, peace, patience, kindness, generosity, faithfulness, gentleness, and self-control" (Galatians 5:22-23) that God has given to us. As a result of God's grace, we become forgiven reconcilers! We forgive others as we have been forgiven and help them become reconciled.

## As servant-leaders

In our *actions*, we will become known as servant-leaders. God gives each of us at least one gift for the benefit of others. As we use the gift, we become a skilled leader in that area of life or work. As Peter writes, "Like good stewards of the manifold grace of God, serve one another with whatever gift each of you has received" (1 Peter 4:10). As we come under the new management of Jesus, our actions and modes of operation change. We turn from being (or admiring) tyrants who "lord it over" others, and seek to become followers of Jesus who "came not to be served but to serve" (Matthew 20:25 and 28). As a result of God's grace and the example of Jesus, we become servant-leaders who use the gifts that God has given us for the benefit of others.

"Intellect, experience, and education all need to be applied to the situation at hand," says Willy Reimer, executive director of the Canadian Conference of Mennonite Brethren Churches. "We are expected to use the spiritual gifts the Holy Spirit has given each of us, gifts intended to bless the community in which we live and serve, gifts such as wisdom, faith, words of knowledge, discernment and prophecy."[12]

## How do we help others to be reconciled and transformed?

Anabaptists see themselves as co-laborers with God in the work of restoring relationships. They believe that God's desire is to "reconcile us to himself through Christ," and that God has "given us the ministry of reconciliation" (2 Corinthians 5:18).

The apostles took Jesus literally when he said, "Go into all the world and preach the good news to all creation. Whoever believes and is baptized will be saved" (Mark 16:15-16 NIV). The apostles helped others become reconciled to God by going to where others were and helping them to make decisions about their lives in relation to Jesus. When persecution forced the apostles out of Jerusalem, they went into all parts of the known world, making disciples and planting churches.

The Christendom that emerged after Constantine did not stress individual decision making and inner transformation as the early church had done. Constantine and other emperors sought to extend the Christian faith and the empire by command and force rather than by inner transformation. Often, faith was in name only.

During the Middle Ages and the Reformation, both Catholic and Protestant leaders believed that the great commission had been fulfilled. They believed that all citizens of their country or province, except Jews and a few others, were Christian. Their main task was to help all citizens to be better Christians through the sacraments and by being more loyal to the rules of the church and its leaders.

Anabaptist Christians rejected this concept of Christianity. They believed every person needed to decide about entering into a voluntary, personal relationship with Jesus Christ. As a result, early Anabaptists, like the early apostles, accepted the great commission as a literal command. Empowered by the Holy Spirit, they became the evangelistic movement of the sixteenth century within Christendom. Historian Franklin Littell writes, "They regarded the real power to be neither in the magistrate nor in the territorial church, but in the Holy Spirit who was dwelling within them. Thus at a time when dominant Protestantism was seeking to get three hundred little states to commit to a territorial determination of their religion, the Anabaptists were sending their missionaries wherever they could get a hearing to preach repentance and the kingdom of God. They believed with the Psalmist that 'the earth is the Lord's, and the fullness thereof . . .' and no land should be forbidden to the proclamation of the gospel."[13]

With persistence and passion, key Anabaptist leaders went throughout Europe seeking to reconcile people to God and to each other.[14] Archivists have found that by the middle of the sixteenth century, Anabaptist missionaries were preaching throughout Germany, Austria, Switzerland, Holland, and France. Several even went as far as Denmark and Sweden in the north and Greece and Constantinople in the south.

It is clear that listeners were invited to make clear decisions and to be baptized upon confession of their new relationship with Jesus. Anabaptist missionary Leonard Bouwens kept a diary in which he recorded the exact date and place of more than ten thousand baptisms he performed! Other Anabaptist preachers also numbered the converts they baptized in the thousands. But even more impressive was the witness of hundreds of ordinary men and women who were so filled with the life of Christ that their relatives, neighbors, and friends were convicted of sin and attracted to the overflowing, transformed life they saw in these believers.[15] Historian Hans Kasdorf observes, "It was not only the leaders who were active in evangelism. There was no distinction between an academically educated ministerial class on the one hand and the laity on the other. Each member was potentially a preacher and a missionary, and each single member had equal opportunity for advancement according to his own competence, just as was the case in the early church."[16]

The cost of obedience, however, was great, and the rapid growth was short-lived. In August 1527, sixty leaders met in Augsburg, Germany, for a missionary conference. They went out as traveling evangelists proclaiming the gospel, baptizing new converts, organizing churches, and establishing new believers in the faith. They were met, however, with intense persecution and death. Only two or three of the original sixty lived to see the fifth year of the movement. The *Ausbund*, a hymnal from that time that the Amish still use in their services, contains short biographical notes of authors listed beside the hymns they wrote, such as "burned 1525"; "drowned 1526"; and "hanged 1527." More than two thousand martyrs are known by name, and estimates are that four or five thousand "men, women, and children fell prey to water, fire and sword."[17]

Unfortunately, because of persecution and the loss of their key leaders, the Anabaptist movement went into retreat. After believers were driven from their homes and villages, they came together in new communities where they lived their faith but were not oriented toward outreach.

Current Anabaptists use a variety of ways to help others become reconciled to God. At an inter-Mennonite consultation on evangelism attended by over two thousand people, representatives gave witness to how seekers had been helped to make decisions to follow Christ through various forms of witness. These forms of witness included peace witness, youth ministries, mass media, social action, drama, music, preaching, education, medical ministries, personal visitation, and small groups.[18]

## What is essential to Anabaptist Christianity?

Anabaptists believe that faith and joyful obedience need to stand together. Seekers need help to decide about their acceptance of God's grace and their willingness to follow Jesus in daily life.

Anabaptists believe that as we open our lives to God's Spirit, our nature (including our thoughts, attitudes, and actions) is changed. This is in contrast to many who believe that their nature remains sinful and have narrowed salvation to a personal spiritual experience or to being a member of a church.

A transformed life is lived in the context of a committed group of followers. Occasional conflicts are bound to occur. When relationships between members become strained, how can they be reconciled to each other? Our next chapter explores how that can and must happen.

## Questions for reflection and discussion

1. What are the offenses that disrupt our relationship with God? How does one become reconciled to God?

2. Reflect on the different ways in which believers in the Christian faith emphasize salvation and reconciliation.

| Many Christians emphasize: | Anabaptists Christians emphasize: |
|---|---|
| Either evangelism or peacemaking is at the center of our work. | Reconciliation is at the center of our work. |
| Being Christian means being a member of a Christian family or church. | Being Christian means accepting God's grace and invitation to joyful obedience. |
| Being saved means being spared an eternity in hell. | Being saved means being reconciled to God and God's family. |
| Salvation means general remission and forgiveness of sin. | Salvation means specific deliverance from sin. |
| Salvation is a personal spiritual experience; our nature remains sinful. | Salvation is a transforming experience; our nature is transformed. |
| Evangelism is a special gift. | Evangelism is the responsibility of all believers. |

3. What were the Anabaptists so passionate about that they could energetically evangelize despite persecution and death?

4. How are you or your church helping to reconcile individuals to God?

# EIGHT

# Members Are Reconciled to Each Other

*When you are offering your gift at the altar, if you
remember that your brother or sister has something against
you, leave your gift there before the altar and go; first be
reconciled to your brother or sister, and then come
and offer your gift.*
*Matthew 5:23-24*

**A S WITH ANY** other organization, the members of a
family or church will at times experience conflict. Jesus,
the disciples, and early Anabaptists all had conflicts, as do
members of all churches and all denominations. The important
point to consider is how believers work out their conflicts and
retain or restore their relationships.

It is important to remember that conflicts may be due to differing personalities, beliefs, goals, regulations, cultures, and styles. Followers of Christ often have legitimate, honest disagreements. Not all conflicts are due to sin. Paul and Barnabas had disagreements about the usefulness of Mark. As a result, two evangelistic teams came into service. No sin was involved (see Acts 15:39-41).

It is important to know that we can disagree without being disagreeable.[1] While conflict resolution focuses on the problem, reconciliation focuses on the relationship. A relationship can be restored even when we are unable to resolve a conflict.

The work of reconciliation seeks to develop healthy relationships between people who are in conflict with each other. When they encounter conflict, followers of Christ are encouraged to "think reconciliation" rather than to decide quickly who is right and who is wrong.

In this chapter, we explore how the church has dealt with conflict and, more specifically, how Anabaptists have reconciled strained or broken relationships within their own ranks.

## How has the church dealt with conflict?

Jesus had to deal with conflict within his primary group of followers. On one occasion, his disciples argued with each other about who would be the greatest in his kingdom (see Luke 9:46-48). At another time the disciples disagreed with Jesus when he decided to go to Jerusalem during the time of the Passover (see Matthew 16:21-23). Jesus was able to use times of disagreement to teach lessons and to build stronger relationships.

Regrettably, throughout much of church history, leaders have chosen to deal with deviant thought and behavior through harsh punishment. Leaders believed that if erring members were punished severely enough, they would change their attitudes, words, and actions. Deviants were seen as criminals who needed to be corrected. Heresy was seen as a capital offense. Catholic authorities preferred to burn heretics at the stake, while Protestants practiced decapitation and drowning.

"What we today call persecution was in the sixteenth century regarded as church discipline," writes historian Walter Klaassen. "Anabaptists were always considered to be members of the church who had gone astray. Church authorities therefore felt responsible for them. The discipline was often severe, involving imprisonment, torture, exile, deprivation of property, and even death. The death sentence as the ultimate act of discipline had a long history. The only way of getting rid of an incorrigible heretic was to put him to death."[2]

## How did early Anabaptists deal with conflict?

Anabaptist leaders took a different approach from both Catholic and Protestant leaders. While they admitted that secular governments might use the sword to settle disputes, they rejected torture, imprisonment, and death as legitimate means of discipline.

Early Anabaptist leaders insisted that the false oaths, violence, drunkenness, and debauchery that the church all too often tolerated needed to be addressed. However, they wanted to address the issues in Christ's way, so instead of harsh punishment they adopted what was called the rule of Christ. The rule of Christ became their primary way of dealing with heretics and those who were no longer following Jesus in daily life.

According to the rule of Christ, as recorded in Matthew 18, if a member of the church engaged in sin or heresy, leaders were to do the following:

1. Talk directly with the person: "If another member of the church sins against you, go and point out the fault when the two of you are alone. If the member listens to you, you have

regained that one" (Matthew 18:15). (We must recognize that in many cultures, such as Eastern ones, a significant intermediary in the family is called on to help resolve a conflict.)

2. Get objective help: "But if you are not listened to, take one or two others along with you, so that every word may be confirmed by the evidence of two or three witnesses" (Matthew 18:16).

3. Take it to the church: "If the member refuses to listen to them, tell it to the church" (Matthew 18:17). Taking it to the church may today mean taking the matter to a meeting of the church council.

4. Let the person go: "And if the offender refuses to listen even to the church, let such a one be to you as a Gentile and a tax collector" (Matthew 18:17). The person is moved from the membership list to the evangelism list as an unbeliever in need of reconciliation.

## What is the reconciliation cycle?

Ron Kraybill, a conflict resolution practitioner, designed a tool called "the reconciliation cycle," which is a way of interpreting and implementing the rule of Christ. It has helped many people learn how to reconcile and be reconciled to each other.

Kraybill, who served as a training adviser to the South African National Peace Accord, based the cycle on his experience in working with people after apartheid was abolished.[3] He and many others, including United Nations personnel, have used it in many other conflict situations.

While conflict resolution is handled differently in different cultures, we will use the "reconciliation cycle" as a basic model for resolving conflict and restoring relationships between persons or groups. Some modifications may be needed according to context and culture.

The seven steps in the reconciliation cycle can be pictured as shown in the diagram.

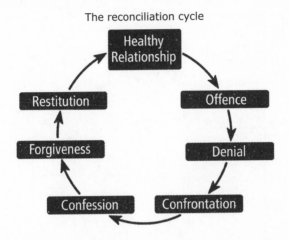

The reconciliation cycle

In chapter 4, I described a situation that arose during my first pastorate between a man I called Vernon, the chair of the congregation, and John, the chair of the elders. As you will recall, Vernon had offended John at a congregational meeting when he said that one of John's suggestions was "stupid." The following describes how Vernon and John were reconciled according to the reconciliation cycle.

1. **Healthy relationship:** Originally, Vernon and John had a healthy relationship. They shared deeply with each other, kept their promises, and experienced a spirit of trust.

2. **Offense:** Vernon offended John by, in a congregational meeting, calling one of John's suggestions "stupid." An offense is any attitude, word, or act that causes harm to another person. The trust and friendship between Vernon and John was broken by the offense to the extent that the two would no longer talk with each other on Sunday mornings.

3. **Denial:** Initially, Vernon denied that he had done anything wrong by saying such things as "It was all in fun"; "I didn't mean anything harmful"; "John is too sensitive." Denial is refusing to tell the truth by excusing, blaming, or acting as if something didn't happen. It offers temporary relief to the offender, but in the long run makes things worse.

4. **Confrontation:** I confronted Vernon with the need for reconciliation and brought the two men together for face-to-face dialogue. I promised that the meeting would take place in a safe environment and that as they shared there would be no interruptions or rebuttals. Confronting, if done in a caring way, helps an offender face the truth.

5. **Confession:** At the face-to-face meeting, I first asked John, the elder who had been offended, to share in an honest and open way his feelings of embarrassment, hurt, and anger. Vernon, the chair, was to listen without rebuttal. While John shared, Vernon came to realize that John's hurt was genuine. In a repentant spirit, he apologized to John by saying, "I realize that not only what I said but how I said it was wrong." Confession is telling the truth about something that was said or done. It often represents the turning point in resolving conflict.

6. **Forgiveness:** Vernon faced John and asked, "Will you forgive me?" After a pause, John extended his hand, and said, "I forgive you." The two men embraced, and the next Sunday were seen talking with each other in the vestibule. Forgiveness is a way of dealing with an offense. It requires an offended person, like John, to absorb the hurt or liability that in reality an offender, like Vernon, should pay. Through offering forgiveness, John became free of the desire for payback or to act in revenge.

7. **Restitution:** At the next congregational meeting, Vernon, with agreement from John, shared with the congregation that he had offended John at the previous meeting and that John had graciously forgiven him. Restitution is making compensation or amends for damage, loss, or injury. The aim of restitution is for the offender to show remorse by attempting to restore the object or relationship to its original condition. Vernon's sharing restored respect for John and affirmed him as a man who was giving commendable spiritual leadership to the congregation.

## What are other patterns for resolving conflict?

In addition to the rule of Christ, the apostles practiced other patterns for resolving conflict. For instance, in Acts 6, when the needs of widows were being overlooked, those responsible studied the problem from all sides and proposed a solution. In this case, the entire community participated in selecting seven people to oversee the food distribution program (see Acts 6:1-7). This resolved the problem.

Later, when there was disagreement about what should be expected of converts from the Gentile world, those concerned met for what has been called the Jerusalem Conference. With the help of Scripture, tradition, the sharing of experiences, and the living presence of Jesus, the council discerned what was essential for becoming a follower of Christ. They decided to be firm on the basics and flexible on the nonessentials (see Acts 15:1-29).

The apostle Paul found that the Corinthian Christians were using secular courts to resolve their conflicts. He asked, "Can it be that there is no one among you wise enough to decide between one believer and another?" (1 Corinthians 6:5). While taking an issue to court may solve a conflict, many have found that it does not restore a relationship.[4] For this reason, it is better to help persons in conflict to work together toward win-win solutions. This calls for them to collaborate in setting and reaching common goals. Relationships need to be nurtured and strengthened throughout any reconciling process.

## How are members held accountable?

Augustine and Luther believed that the true church was invisible to humans. Only God could tell who was a true believer. Anabaptists, however, believed that by observing attitudes, words, and actions, it was possible to discern who were followers of Christ and who were not. They expected high ethical standards of members and wanted to hold each other and especially their leaders accountable to their promises. Those who were being unfaithful to their baptismal vows or to the standards of the church were disciplined according to the rule of Christ.

Currently in Anabaptist circles, candidates for baptism or membership transfer are asked to make promises to which they will be held accountable. Questions such as the following are asked:

- Have you renounced the evil powers of Satan and this world and turned to Jesus Christ as your Lord and Savior?

- Do you desire to be received as a member of this congregation on the basis of its congregational covenant?

- Are you willing to give and receive counsel in the context of this congregation?

- Are you ready to participate in the mission of this church?

- If a brother or sister is in need, are your goods available to them?[5]

The congregation then covenants with the new member or members by making a statement such as the following.

As we now receive you into the fellowship of the church, we make this covenant with you as we renew our own covenant with God: to bear one another's burdens, to assist in times of need, to share our gifts and possessions, to forgive as Christ has forgiven us, to support each other in joy and sorrow, and in all things to work for the common good, thus making known Christ's presence among us to the glory of God.[6]

In early Anabaptist times, communion was a time for members to be held accountable for the promises they had made at baptism or upon becoming members. A separate pre-service was held in which members were asked to examine themselves in regard to their fellowship with God and each other. Those who were not living according to their promises, and did not alter their ways, received pastoral counsel, admonition, or both. In extreme cases, they received "the ban," which meant that they were excluded from fellowship with members until a new commitment was made.

Unfortunately, while helping members to examine their lives, pastors and bishops often became judgmental. In *The Naked Anabaptist*, Stuart Murray notes, "Anabaptists today, rightly cautious because of abuses in this area, nevertheless want to nurture and develop churches where mutual accountability is understood, practiced, and valued. Mutual accountability is an antidote to gossip and backbiting, a defense against factions and divisions, and a resource for spiritual growth. . . . When relationships break down, there is a process to bring healing and restoration."[7]

"Discipline comes from the same root word as to disciple," says Marlin Jeschke, a contemporary proponent of appropriate church discipline. "In the same way that *evangelism* aims to make disciples of those who have not become Christian by bringing them into the community, so *discipline* seeks to restore to the community those who have strayed."[8]

I well remember my father, who was a church board member, making a personal visit to a relatively new member named Ron. Ron had missed communion for three times in a row. My father explored the reasons and tried to restore him to community.

"The goal of all healthy discipline in the church is to enable people to be better disciples of Jesus Christ," says Ervin Stutzman, executive director of Mennonite Church USA. "Discipline rarely works unless the person being disciplined is genuinely seeking to become a better Christian."[9]

## What is essential to Anabaptist Christianity?

Early Anabaptists saw the church as a uniquely covenanted group of believers who had been reconciled to God and to each other. They sought to hold each other accountable to the commitments they had made to God and each other at baptism.

Early Anabaptists adopted the rule of Christ as their basic guideline for discipline in the church. This was in contrast to the prevailing church, which generally used penal punishment as a way of forcing deviant members to change. In the best of times, communion has prompted experiences of joy because participants are celebrating and giving thanks that they have been forgiven not only by God but also by those participating in the communion experience.

In addition to helping individuals to be reconciled to God and to each other, the ministry of reconciliation calls us to work at reconciling conflicted people in the world. This is the focus of our next chapter.

## Questions for reflection and discussion

1. What story can you tell of two people or groups who were in conflict at one time and have now been reconciled? Were the steps of either the rule of Christ or the reconciliation cycle used?

2. Discuss the following attitudes that believers in Christ hold in relationship to reconciling members to one another.

| Many Christians emphasize: | Anabaptists Christians emphasize: |
|---|---|
| Deciding who is right and who is wrong in a conflict. | Seeking to "think reconciliation" when dealing with conflict. |
| Punishing wrongdoers in the hope they will change. | Helping wrongdoers to confess clearly what was said or done. |
| Enacting tougher laws and having stricter enforcement. | Holding members accountable for the promises they have made. |
| Inviting all to participate in communion. | Inviting participants to examine their relationships with God and others. |

3. What is the purpose of confronting an offender? When is it important to do so?

4. Why does going to court often fail to restore a relationship?

# NINE

# Conflicts in the World Are Reconciled

*Though we live in the world, we do not wage war as the world does. The weapons we fight with are not the weapons of the world.*

*2 Corinthians 10:3-4 NIV*

**W**HILE MANY Christians see peacebuilding as being an optional add-on to the gospel, Anabaptist Christians see it as being at the heart of the gospel. Jesus, who is the Prince of Peace and the center of our faith, is the reason why reconciliation is at the center of our work. "Through him God was pleased to reconcile to himself all things, whether on earth or in heaven, by making peace through the blood of his cross" (Colossians 1:20).

From their beginnings, being peaceful and working for peace has characterized the Anabaptists. "We are a peace church because we are first and foremost a Jesus church" says

Bruxy Cavey, teaching pastor of a multisite church in Ontario. "Jesus leads us in the way of peace. We care about reconciliation because Jesus cares about reconciliation. We care about justice because we care about Jesus."[1]

In this chapter we explore how Jesus, the early Christians, and the early Anabaptists sought to reconcile conflict. We will contrast their peacebuilding approaches with those who choose violence. Special attention will be given to how contemporary Anabaptist-minded people are seeking to do peacebuilding.

## How did Jesus relate to conflict?

The Jews had expected their Messiah to come as a violent, revolutionary leader who would set things right by destroying evildoers and their unjust ways. Jesus, however, came as the Prince of Peace, saying, "love your enemies and pray for those who persecute you, so that you may be children of your Father in heaven" (Matthew 5:43-45a).

"Blessed are the peacemakers, for they will be called children of God" (Matthew 5:9), Jesus said. He instructed his followers, "Do not resist an evildoer. But if anyone strikes you on the right cheek, turn the other also; and if anyone wants to sue you and take your coat, give your cloak as well; and if anyone forces you to go one mile, go also the second mile" (Matthew 5:39-41). Jesus introduced the idea that we are transformed in our attitudes and actions toward conflict by inner regeneration.

"Christian peacemaking must balance an emphasis on God's initiative with a call for human response," says Mennonite leader Ervin Stutzman. "Such peace is brought about only through God's divine action to bring about transformation in human life and social interaction."[2]

Jesus saw the kingdom of God as a kingdom of peaceful relationships that would be quite different from the kingdoms of this world. When Pilate asked him whether he was seeking to be "King of the Jews," Jesus said, "My kingdom is not from this world. If my kingdom were from this world, my followers would be fighting" (John 18:36).

Jesus demonstrated a special attitude of peacebuilding during his crucifixion and death. "It was precisely the cross . . . the failure of Christ in the world . . . which led to his success in history," observed Dietrich Bonhoeffer, a German advocate for discipleship.[3] Jesus exposed and overcame evil by allowing himself to be killed rather than to kill. In this way, he demonstrated a new way of overcoming sin and the principalities and powers of those controlled by Satan. Through his life, death, and resurrection, he transformed the hearts of human beings and empowered them to live as he had lived.

The apostle Peter encouraged new believers to follow the example of Jesus. "When he was abused, he did not return abuse; when he suffered, he did not threaten" (1 Peter 2:23a).

## How did early Christians relate to conflict?

Jesus delegated to his followers the task of reconciling conflict. "All this is from God," says Paul in 2 Corinthians 5:18, "who reconciled us to himself through Christ, and has given us the ministry of reconciliation."

The apostle Paul followed in the footsteps of Jesus by saying, "Never avenge yourselves. . . . 'If your enemies are hungry, feed them; if they are thirsty, give them something to drink; for by doing this you will heap burning coals on their heads.' Do not be overcome by evil, but overcome evil with good" (Romans 12:19-21).

One of the greatest challenges facing the apostle Paul and the early church was to reconcile Jews and Gentiles to each other. The people from these two groups were in severe conflict with each other, but when members from these two groups became reconciled to Christ, they also came to peace with each other. Early Christians could say triumphantly of their churches, "There is neither Jew nor Greek, neither slave nor free, nor is there male and female, for you are all one in Christ Jesus" (Galatians 3:28 NIV).

Despite wars and rumors of war, early Christians were committed to peace. To our knowledge, no followers of Jesus were engaged in military combat during the first two hundred years of church history. It appears as if reconciliation instead of armed conflict was at the center of their work.

But changes occurred when church and state were combined. Emperors, who were warriors, soon expected Christians to fight evil like everyone else. A little over a century later, in 416 CE, only people of Christian heritage were allowed in the army.[4]

Augustine tried to find a way to justify the participation of Christians in violent conflict by developing a set of guidelines now called the just war theory. Many Christians today believe that if the moral requirements of just war theory were carefully followed, there would be few, if any, wars. However, from their beginnings, Anabaptists pointed out many problems with this theory. For example:

- While the theory states that "war must be for a just or right cause," inevitably, both sides will see their side as being just.

- The theory assumes that evil can be overcome with violence, but history proves that violence leads to more violence. Violence must be overcome with *non*violence.

- The theory states that war is justified if it is a last resort. However, research indicates there have always been alternatives to war.[5] Highest honor should be given to those who prevent war.

Stuart Murray points out that churches that espouse the just war theory usually also celebrate the warring efforts of their governments: "For many centuries churches have endorsed lethal violence, blessed the weapons of war, prayed for military success, celebrated victories in acts of worship, and deployed missionaries under the protection of conquering armies."[6]

Anabaptists believe that Christians need to say a firm "No!" to participation in violence and war. Although violence makes sense according to the logic of the world, Christians belong to Christ, who transforms us and clearly calls us to live in another way. Jesus was clear: people who follow him are not to kill or destroy. Transformed people do not do such things!

## How did early Anabaptists relate to conflict?

From the beginning, Anabaptist believers took a stand against violence. Like the early disciples, most early Anabaptists refused to join the military, even though Muslim Turks were trying to invade Europe and were at the gates of Vienna. Anabaptists were convinced that believers should not "take the sword" or inflict suffering on others. Enduring suffering was preferable to inflicting suffering or to taking the life of a pursuer.

Regrettably, a group of radical Anabaptists was not committed to nonviolence. In 1534, these extremists wrongfully and forcefully took over the city of Münster. In their attempt to rule, they used violence and introduced a system of dominance. The Münster Rebellion, as it was later called, lasted until June 1535, when the city was recaptured by the former ruling authorities. The action of these extremists gave Anabaptists a bad reputation that in some circles has lasted until the present time.

By 1540, Anabaptist believers had come to a wide consensus that reborn, baptized Christians must refuse to participate in violence.[7] Anabaptists believed they must do what Jesus would do if he were in their situation. This was in sharp contrast to Augustine, Martin Luther, and others who believed Christians needed to be obedient to government when it called them to go to war.

During the American Revolution and Civil War, many Anabaptist believers paid a special tax to the government or found other ways to be exempt from military duty. In the nineteenth and twentieth centuries, many conscientious objectors left Russia and other European lands to resettle in North or South American countries where they were promised alternatives to military service.

During World War I, conscientious objectors in North America were often ridiculed and imprisoned for refusing induction into armed service. Some of their churches were burned, and several conscientious objectors were tortured until they died. During subsequent wars, agreements were reached that allowed conscientious objectors to choose alternative service.

## How do various groups of people relate to conflict?

In our day, people seek to overcome or defeat those with whom they have conflict in at least five ways, as illustrated in the chart on page 144. It becomes obvious that people see evil differently and therefore seek to defeat or overcome it in contrasting ways. The approaches for overcoming conflict might be described as follows.

*Terrorists* see the leaders or values of a prevailing or invading system as being evil or unjust. From their viewpoint, the dominant system is "fallen." Since status quo leaders are not willing to voluntarily give up their values or power, terrorists use violence to defeat them. Led by extremists, they seek to overthrow the present system via violent revolution. They may say, "Some people need to die."

*Militarists* see the violent, revolutionary actions of terrorists and criminals as evil. Under the direction of trained officers, they seek to defeat or overcome their violence with greater violence. Sadly, a deep understanding of enemy views and values is often lacking. Basic training for combat is generally opposed to the spirit of Christ and his teaching.[8] Traditionally, Anabaptists have said that a secular government may need to use violence to defeat evil, but Christians should not be involved in it. They believe violence, even counterviolence, often leads to more violence.

*Pacifists* say a clear no to violence and the taking of human life. Anabaptists have historically been known for withdrawing from conflict. This includes from participation in military operations or even from secular government. For many current Anabaptists, pacifism is too passive. Many have moved from strict nonresistance toward nonviolent action against evil.

*Peacebuilders* say no to war and violence but go one step further. They actively seek to correct injustice and eliminate the causes of violence. Their goal is to bring about a peaceful revolution by addressing inequalities, showing compassion, and implementing programs of restorative justice that transform enemies into friends.

*Spiritual warriors* place their trust in the justice and power of God to overcome evil powers. Through such practices as prayer, fasting, exorcism, and the laying on of hands, they trust that God's grace and power will change the hearts and attitudes of the people causing the conflict.

Anabaptist leaders have been convinced that we are to be peacebuilders. We are to fight evil as vigorously—or even more vigorously—than anyone else, but we are to fight *differently*. With the apostle Paul we say, "For though we live in the world, we do not wage war as the world does. The weapons we fight with are not the weapons of the world. On the contrary, they

**How people relate to conflict**

| | Terrorist | Military | Pacifist | Peacemaker | Spiritual warriors |
|---|---|---|---|---|---|
| **Their strategy** | Violent revolutionary | Anti-revolutionary | Anti-military-industrial-complex | Peaceful revolutionary | Pray, exercise demons, the laying on of hands |
| **Their motto** | "Some people need to die." | "Protect the status quo." | "Violence creates more violence." | "Overcome evil with good." | "Stand still. God will fight the battle." |
| **Their attitude towards violence** | **Yes** to violence | **Yes** to violence | **No** to violence and injustice | **Yes** to love and restorative justice | **No** to violence |
| **Their leaders** | **Extremists** are in command | **Generals** are in command | **Conscience** is in command | **Jesus' principles** are in command | **Spiritual warriors** |

have divine power to demolish strongholds" (2 Corinthians 10:3-4 NIV).

Following are three primary ways in which current Anabaptists are seeking to overcome evil and the conflict that it causes. These are *nonviolent action, restorative justice,* and *alternative service.*

## How is conflict reconciled through nonviolent action?

Jesus practiced nonviolent action when he led thousands of his followers into Jerusalem on a donkey instead of on a white horse. A donkey was known as a servant animal in contrast to a white horse, which was associated with military power (see Matthew 21:1-11). Jesus did not initiate conflict.

Early Christians and early Anabaptists lived their faith even when they were persecuted, driven from their homes, and even killed. They continued to live nonviolently when faced with the prospect of being burned at the stake. They chose to suffer rather than cause others to suffer. As people observed the character of these believers, their solid nonviolent witness became the seed of the church. Despite persecution the church grew rapidly.

Ronald J. Sider, founder and president emeritus of Evangelicals for Social Action, notes, "Mahatma Gandhi's nonviolent revolution defeated the British Empire and . . . Martin Luther King Jr.'s peaceful civil rights crusade changed American history. There have been scores upon scores of instances of nonviolent victories over dictatorship and oppression in the past one hundred years. Recent scholarship has shown that nonviolent revolutions against injustice and dictatorship are actually more successful than violent campaigns." [9]

Nonviolent action refers to a variety of methods or strategies. Gene Sharp, today the foremost scholar on nonviolence, describes 198 tactics of nonviolent action.[10] These include verbal and symbolic persuasion through social, economic, and political noncooperation, including boycotts and strikes, and even more confrontational but nonviolent intervention.

"Nonviolent action is not the same as passive nonresistance," clarifies Sider. "Coercion is not necessarily violent. Nonlethal coercion, as in a boycott or peaceful march that respects the integrity and personhood of the 'opponent,' is not immoral or violent. It seeks both to end the oppression and to reconcile the oppressor through nonviolent methods."[11]

A small but prominent example of nonviolent action is the Christian Peacemaker Teams movement. Christian Peacemaker Teams have gone to places of high tension such as Iraq, Ireland, Palestine, and Colombia to stand between conflicted groups. In doing so, they prevent violence and build bridges to peace. The movement currently has about thirty full-time activists in various locations and more than 150 trained reservists who are available in times of acute need.[12]

In Colombia, a company called Daabon had confiscated local farmers' lands to grow palm oil being used by the Body Shop, a company that promotes itself as ethical and "green." After a year and a half of nonviolent pressure by Christian Peacemaker Team members, which involved nonviolent direct action in stores, a letter-writing campaign, and an economic boycott, the Body Shop canceled its contract, the Daabon company pulled out, and the farmers got their land back.[13]

## How is conflict reconciled through restorative justice?

Restorative justice aims to put things right in the world so there can be peace. Pope Paul VI gave emphasis to this way of working for peace by proclaiming, "If you want to work for peace, work for justice!"[14]

The Victim-Offender Reconciliation Program (VORP), begun by Mennonites in North America, is one example of seeking to resolve conflict through restorative justice. One example of the VORP process involves that of a young man, whom we will call Rick, who was arrested for stealing Scott's car. The judge wanted to prevent poverty-stricken Rick from getting into further crime, so he assigned the case to the local Victim-Offender Reconciliation Program. A VORP volunteer talked privately first with Rick, then with Scott, inviting them to seek resolution of the conflict by meeting face-to-face to discuss details of the conflict and how it might be resolved. Meeting each other across the same table, the VORP volunteer asked Rick, the offender, to share in detail and without interruption exactly when, how, and why he had stolen Scott's car and what he had done with it. The volunteer then asked Scott, the victim, to share with Rick the feelings of bewilderment, anger, frustration, and loss that he and his family had experienced as a result of the crime.

Rick responded to Scott's pain in the form of an apology and with a desire to make things right. The VORP volunteer helped Rick and Scott to explore ways that would lead to justice, which resulted in Rick agreeing to pay for the mileage he had driven in Scott's car, to do forty hours of community service, and to attend a series of financial planning classes. The VORP volunteer presented the judge with a report of the dialogue and the agreed-upon conditions of reconciliation. The judge in this case decided that justice would be served by the conditions. He assigned a probation officer to check in at two-week intervals to assure that the agreements made between Rick and Scott were being fulfilled. If not, a one-year jail sentence for Rick would begin.

One school system that has used restorative justice rather than punitive punishment experienced a 40 percent drop in suspensions. More than 88 percent of the teachers involved said that the restorative justice practices were either very or some-what helpful in managing difficult behavior.[15] Other research has confirmed that using a restorative justice model with youth who have been in trouble at school has had a significant impact on behavior, graduation rates, and absenteeism.

## How is conflict reconciled through alternative service?

At various times and places Mennonites have negotiated agreements with governments that allowed conscientious objectors to perform alternative service that contributed to the nation's welfare. This was true in the United States and Canada during World War II. Alternative service is a way of working for peace or in peaceful endeavors when others are required to go to war.

During World War II, 34.5 million men in the United States registered for the draft. Of those, 72,354 applied for conscientious objector status. Of these, about 25,000 served in noncombatant roles; 27,000 failed to pass the physical exam and were exempt; more than 6,000 rejected the draft outright and chose to go to jail instead of serving the war effort; and 12,000 chose to perform alternative service. Ten thousand of these were from Mennonite, Quaker, and Brethren backgrounds. Supervised by the Civilian Public Service program, they served in alternate ways in hospitals, national parks, forests, farms, and mines. These services benefited the country while not violating the basic beliefs of the participants about the taking of life.[16]

Alternative service to the military led to a variety of programs and services that continue to alleviate suffering and work for justice. For example, during the early stages of the Vietnam War, I, as an American citizen, was called to serve my country and was classified I-A, which meant ready for combat duty. Because of my commitment to Christ, I appealed to the government and was reclassified I-O, which granted me the opportunity to serve my country and my God as the director of a mobile clinic in Taiwan. The team was composed of a doctor, dentist, nurse, and evangelist. In the process of going village to village offering basic healthcare, we made thousands of friends. When a high-ranking American military advisor heard my story, he shook his head and said, "We are losing the war in Vietnam because we cannot win the friendship of the village people. You COs [conscientious objectors] could win it better than we!"[17] These experiences have helped me and others to believe that by committing ourselves to following Jesus and his ways, we can do as much or more for peace than if we were to serve in the military.

More recently, a few other countries have developed options for performing national alternative service instead of military service. Sadly, many countries have not. Anabaptist conscientious objectors in Korea and Colombia have been imprisoned for refusing to serve in the military.

Anabaptist churches around the world have established more than sixty service programs and networks that seek to alleviate suffering and bring justice. These include Meserete Kristos Relief and Development, Malawi Passion Center for Children, Mennonite Christian Service Fellowship of India, and Comité de Desarrollo Social of Honduras.[18]

North American examples of programs that emerged out of alternative service include:

- **Mennonite Central Committee:** MCC began as a response to the starvation of Mennonite families in the Ukraine due to war. It has become known worldwide for its relief, development, and peace work "in the name of Christ." It serves with many partners around the world to alleviate poverty and injustice which are often seeds of conflict and war.

- **Mennonite Health Services:** When conscientious objectors saw the deplorable treatment of the mentally ill where they served, they established a series of mental health centers based on the values of Christian love and compassion. These have been in the national interest.

- **Pax:** Mennonite Central Committee administered the Pax (Latin for peace) program, which enabled more than twelve hundred conscientious objectors to serve in Germany, Austria, Algeria, and forty other countries. They constructed homes for refugees, built roads, worked in agricultural improvement, and more. Pax was a prototype that helped influence the formation of the U.S. Peace Corps program.

- **Teachers Abroad Program:** More than one thousand teachers between 1962 and the mid-1980s went to ten African countries, Jamaica, and Bolivia to teach in local schools, organized through MCC. Later, many leaders came from the schools where they taught. The TAP program was the forerunner of other educational ventures both in North America and around the world.

- **Mennonite Conciliation Services:** MCS was a program of MCC that pioneered conciliation work for Mennonites in the U.S. in response to forces in society that contribute to poverty, injustice, and violence. Growing from this experience, Mennonites developed training institutes at Mennonite colleges, universities, and local community peace centers.

- **Peace Education and Advocacy:** The Peace and Justice Network of Mennonite Church USA grew out of the longstanding peace resourcing work of the denomination and predates MCS. The MCC peace offices in Washington,

D.C., and Ottawa, Canada, focus on witnessing for peace with these respective governments and policy-makers.

"As ambassadors, we do not come with a spirit of power and triumphalism," writes Laura Kalmar, former associate director of communications for Mennonite Central Committee Canada, about alternative service workers. "We seek to come in humility and weakness as fallible human beings. We bear God's image in imperfect vessels—our words fail, our actions fall short and our knowledge is incomplete. And yet, somewhere between the cracks and imperfections, the light of God shines through to a dark world."[19]

With the absence of a draft in the United States and Canada, fewer individuals are currently performing alternative-type service. Many Anabaptists are concerned that the peace position is eroding.

## What is essential to Anabaptist Christianity?

Anabaptist Christians, upon the basis of Scripture and the example of Jesus, say a clear no to violence. We are to overcome conflict by removing injustice and by showing love. By treating enemies in the spirit of Jesus, we seek to turn them into friends. This is in contrast to those who seek to resolve conflict through violence.

In his great commission, Jesus charged us to teach new believers "everything that I have commanded you" (Matthew 28:20). Christ's commands include teaching the ways of peace. Teaching nonviolence and peace should be part of every discipleship and membership training class. Anabaptist colleges and seminaries need to be commended for forming peace and conflict studies programs.

Reconciling conflict is hard work. Refraining from engaging in violence may require us to lose our reputations, property, or even our lives—as was true for Jesus, the early Christians, and the early Anabaptists. However, there is no greater joy than to live a reconciled life and to bring others into honest, reconciled relationships.

From where comes the power to live a life of discipleship and peace as described in these first nine chapters? This is the subject of chapter 10.

## Questions for reflection and discussion

1.  What has been your experience and the experience of your family in relationship to war?

2.  Discuss the following perspectives in reference to the just war theory and Christian peacemaking.

| Just war advocates emphasize: | Christian peacemakers emphasize: |
| --- | --- |
| Proper authorities may need to declare war. | Secular authorities may need to declare war, but Christians should not participate in it. |
| Evil can be overcome with redemptive violence. | Violence leads to more violence. |
| War is justified when it is a last resort. | There have always been alternatives to war. |
| Governments are responsible when the lives of enemies are taken. | Each person is responsible for his or her own actions. |

3.  What steps might you take to work for greater peace, justice, and reconciliation in your community?

# Conclusions

# TEN

# The Holy Spirit's Work Is Essential

*You will receive power when the Holy Spirit has come upon you; and you will be my witnesses in Jerusalem, in all Judea and Samaria, and to the ends of the earth.*

*Acts 1:8*

**WHO OR WHAT** gave the early Anabaptists a new vision for the church? What prompted them to begin baptizing upon the profession of faith? From where did they receive the courage and strength to face opposition and endure severe persecution?

While early Anabaptist Christians introduced many unique theological and organizational views, many historians and scholars have overlooked the fact that perhaps the most essential aspect of the Anabaptist movement was its emphasis on the Holy Spirit. Mennonite Brethren leader J. B. Toews once said, "Correct theology, even Anabaptist theology, without experiential knowledge of Christ through the Holy Spirit leaves the church impotent."[1]

In chapter 7, we explored how the work of the Holy Spirit transforms the thoughts, emotions, and actions of those who open their lives to the grace of God. In this chapter we will further focus on the work of the Holy Spirit in the life and ministry of Jesus, the apostles, and the early Anabaptists, and in many churches today.

The Holy Spirit can be seen as the central hub to our understanding of Jesus, community, and reconciliation, as depicted in the diagram.

**The place of the Holy Spirit**

There is a common denominator between what happened in and through the life and ministry of Jesus, the early church, the Anabaptist movement, and what is happening in many churches today. That common denominator is the transforming presence and work of the Holy Spirit.

## What is essential to an understanding of Jesus?

For centuries, people have wondered how Jesus could be both human and divine. A key understanding is that while Jesus was fully human, he was also filled with the Spirit of God. A person is known by their spirit. The Scriptures, especially the gospel of Luke, repeatedly emphasize the relationship of Jesus and the Holy Spirit. Note the following (emphasis mine):

As [Jesus] was praying, the heavens opened, and the *Holy Spirit* . . . descended on him like a dove (Luke 3:21-22 NLT).

Then Jesus, full of the *Holy Spirit* . . . was led by the Spirit in the wilderness, where he was tempted by the devil for forty days (Luke 4:1-2 NLT).

Jesus returned to Galilee, filled with the *Holy Spirit's* power (Luke 4:14 NLT).

He unrolled the scroll and found the place where this was written: "The *Spirit of the Lord* is upon me, for he has anointed me to bring Good News to the poor. He has sent me to proclaim that captives will be released, that the blind will see, that the oppressed will be set free, and that the time of the Lord's favor has come" (Luke 4:17-19 NLT).

Jesus shouted, "Father, I entrust my spirit into your hands!" And with those words he breathed his last (Luke 23:46 NLT).

Twenty-four times the Gospels refer to people being amazed by the presence and power of God that was evident in Jesus. Luke 5:26 (NLT) says, "Everyone was gripped with great wonder and awe, and they praised God, exclaiming, 'We have seen amazing things today!'"

## What was essential for effective ministry?

At Pentecost, the same Spirit that was in Jesus came upon the apostles. In their ministries, they did exactly what Jesus had been doing. They proclaimed good news to the poor. They healed the sick and released people from bondage. They also received the same type of amazing response from people that Jesus had received. Because of what God did through the apostles, Luke reports that "awe came upon everyone" (Acts 2:43).

Anabaptists also took interest in the presence and work of the Holy Spirit. Historian Peter Klassen observes that throughout the early Anabaptist movement, "there was a profound conviction that the Holy Spirit was at the center of Christian experience. The work of the Holy Spirit enabled the followers of Christ to rise above legalism to the transforming life of joyful obedience."[2]

The Anabaptist movement can rightfully be called the charismatic or Holy Spirit movement of the sixteenth century.[3] In this movement, transformation or salvation began with individual confession of sin and a desire to receive the Holy Spirit. Transformed believers were experience-oriented. Wherever they went, they shared about experiences of what God was doing in their lives and ministries. Perhaps some went overboard. They preached often from Mark 16:17-18, where it says, "And these signs will accompany those who believe: by using my name they will cast out demons; they will speak in new tongues; they will pick up snakes in their hands, and if they drink any deadly thing, it will not hurt them; they will lay their hands on the sick, and they will recover."

The Anabaptist movement came in the midst of the rationalism that was sweeping through Europe. It was a time when reason took priority over revelation. Intellectuals and those of influence believed that everything needed to be reasoned out in rational ways. Among the primary reformers, reasoned belief was of paramount importance; heresy (wrong belief) was punishable with death. In the midst of this mentality, the strong emphasis of the early Anabaptists on the Holy Spirit was rather striking. Menno Simons said, "It is the Holy Spirit that frees us from sin, gives us boldness and makes us cheerful, peaceful, pious and holy." [4]

It was not merely their unique theology of the church and their strong commitment to peace that made the difference in how Anabaptists were perceived. Anabaptists gave a much higher place to the Holy Spirit than did Martin Luther, Ulrich Zwingli, John Calvin, and others. People noticed that there was a marked difference in how transformed Anabaptists lived their lives. They became known as people who lived what they believed even when it meant persecution and death. Pride was turned into humility, lying into honesty, hatred into love, and fear into boldness.

Early Anabaptists believed the Holy Spirit is the agent who brings a new start to people's lives. "It was the coming of the Holy Spirit into their experience that made the difference," observes theologian Walter Klaassen. "The important thing for them was how the Holy Spirit worked in the life of the believer and the church." [5]

## How is the Holy Spirit received?

What might we learn from the early Anabaptists? What steps did they take to receive the Holy Spirit?

It appears that receiving Jesus as Lord and Savior and receiving the Holy Spirit had much in common. In many cases it may have been the same experience or process. It began with desire for the presence of God. Jesus promised his followers that if they asked, this desire would be fulfilled. He said, "If you then, who are evil, know how to give good gifts to your children, how much more will the heavenly Father give the Holy Spirit to those who ask him!" (Luke 11:13). As with Jesus and the apostles, their first step was prayer. The original Pentecost experience happened after forty days of prayer.

Early accounts tell us there was considerable attention given to repentance of known sin both in the early church and in the Anabaptist movement. The apostle Peter explained this condition to the crowd at Pentecost by saying, "Repent, and be baptized every one of you in the name of Jesus Christ so that your sins may be forgiven; and you will receive the gift of the Holy Spirit" (Acts 2:38).

Inner cleansing was combined with an openness and an eagerness toward receiving the Holy Spirit into their lives. Receiving the Holy Spirit was the same as receiving the living presence of Jesus into their inner realities. "The demand is for an inside job," says Richard A. Foster in *Celebration of Discipline*, "and only God can work from the inside. We cannot attain or earn the righteousness of the kingdom of God. It is a grace that is given."[6]

## What might we learn from the Global South?

During the first seventy-five years of the twentieth century, most denominations—including Mennonite, Mennonite Brethren, Brethren in Christ, and other Anabaptist groups—sent hundreds of missionaries to the ends of the earth. Schools and hospitals were established in order to show the love of Christ. By translating the Bible into a number of languages and teaching it as clearly as possible, Anabaptist missionaries built solid foundations.

The globalization of the Christian faith began through the missionary movement and has continued. There are now Anabaptist Christians in more than eighty countries of the world. In 1978, two-thirds of all Anabaptists were in North America and Europe; the remaining third was elsewhere. Today those proportions are reversed, with two-thirds of Anabaptists residing in the Global South. The number of Anabaptist believers in Asia has increased from 75,000 in 1978 to 430,000 in 2015. Even greater increases, from 85,000 to 740,000, have been experienced in Africa. The number of believers in Latin America has also grown exponentially.[7]

The missionary era might be seen as a period of instruction similar to what the disciples received from Jesus. While the missionaries built solid foundations through faithful, Spirit-led teaching and service work, something unusual and extra happened when the Holy Spirit came upon them. Jesus had told the apostles to wait until the Spirit would come in a new way. The Holy Spirit would fill them with power and they would become effective witnesses "in Jerusalem, in all Judea and Samaria, and to the ends of the earth" (Acts 1:8). That happened as Jesus said it would. Rapid growth happened after the departure of Jesus. Phenomenal growth in Anabaptism has also taken place after most of the missionaries went home during the 1970s and early 1980s.

An openness to the Holy Spirit has given new power and effectiveness to those who were brought to a basic relationship with Christ through the early missionaries. National workers can now say with Jesus, "'The *Spirit of the Lord* is upon me, for he has anointed me to bring Good News to the poor. He has sent me to proclaim that captives will be released, that the blind will see, that the oppressed will be set free, and that the time of the Lord's favor has come'" (Luke 4:18-19 NLT, emphasis mine).

Many Anabaptist pastors in the Global South have a keen desire for the presence and work of the Holy Spirit. They spend two or three hours—and sometimes five or more—in prayer to prepare for the preaching of a sermon. Soloists, choir members, and worship leaders might do the same.

An emphasis on the Holy Spirit does not replace teaching the Scriptures. Teaching continues to be central for Spirit-filled believers in the Global South. When asked how Meserete Kristos Church (MKC) congregations are different from other evangelical churches, one Ethiopian pastor told me, "We are the teaching church!"

The transforming work of the Holy Spirit also becomes visible through acts of service. In addition to seven hundred churches, MKC has ministries and congregations in forty prisons. Through these ministries, patterns of revenge killing among the village peoples have largely been broken. So great has been the change in inmates' lives that an invitation has been extended by prison wardens and the Ethiopian government to MKC to begin ministries in all the country's prisons.

The presence of the Holy Spirit also causes verbal witness to be effective. Many churches that emphasize the Holy Spirit are growing by 10 to 12 percent per year. Nearly every growing church in the Global South has an evangelist. This evangelist is often a new convert who is given a small wage to be a witness and to follow up on the witnessing of the congregation's members. The MKC denomination added sixteen thousand new members in 2015.

## Can this happen in the Global North?

The surprising response to the gospel in Africa, Asia, and Latin America is partially related to worldviews that include strong belief in the spirit world. This is as it was in the days of Jesus and the early church. During the week, people live in a world in which they believe evil spirits are active. On Sunday, they come to church and are delighted to learn that Jesus and the Holy Spirit are stronger than those spirits. They tell stories of how relatives have been healed through prayer, how friends have overcome depression, and how neighbors have been transformed.

Anabaptists in the Global North might question whether this kind of faith and spirit is also possible in their churches. Somewhat defensively they might say, "We live in a rational, scientific world; a world in which everything needs to be tested and reasoned out. People in the Global South are much more immersed in the spirit world."

While this is true, we must remember that the early Anabaptists also lived in the midst of the age of reason and yet experienced the renewing and empowering presence and work of the Holy Spirit. It appears that if there is to be a healthy, vibrant faith, there needs to be a balance between reason and revelation.

Author David Wiebe admits that for most contemporary Anabaptists in the Global North, "The work of the Holy Spirit has received 'scant attention' from Mennonites since the Radical Reformation. Perhaps, in our zeal to be Christocentric, we have minimized the Holy Spirit. Embracing the work of the Spirit, who was sent by Christ himself, will not make Anabaptists less Christocentric, but more so." [8]

In fact, many in the Global North who are looking for a deeper or more engaging faith are being attracted through reason to Anabaptist faith. People are finding it reasonable to believe in nonviolent action and peacebuilding. They are finding it reasonable to interpret the Scriptures through the eyes of Jesus. It is reasonable to believe that both forgiveness and joyful obedience are needed for salvation. As a result, many from various backgrounds are being drawn to Anabaptist expressions of faith and life.

While we rejoice in seeing the work of the Holy Spirit, we do well to heed the warning of Arthur Duck, president of *Faculdade Fidelis* Seminary in Brazil, who says, "When we talk about the Holy Spirit, we are often not really concerned with the Holy Spirit, but with what the Spirit can give us—power. . . . This question already appears in the Gospels when Jewish leaders wanted Jesus to perform a miracle before them (Matthew 12:39), or when Herod wished to be entertained with a miracle (Luke 23:8-9)." [9]

A healthy emphasis on both our uniquely reasoned theology and our experiential trust in the Holy Spirit are needed to bring people to authentic faith and life in Christ. New opportunities to learn from each other are presenting themselves as immigrants from Global South churches plant churches next to established churches in the Global North. This presents opportunities for interaction and mutual help that can result in experiences of transformation.

All believers, both in the North and in the South, need to be encouraged in the knowledge that Jesus promised to send us a Helper who would be an advocate, intercessor, comforter, and teacher in times of need (see John 14:16, 26; Romans 8:26-27). We might think of the Holy Spirit as our senior partner. The Holy Spirit provides the resources that we, the junior partners, need in order to make disciples and reconcile conflicts.

## What is essential to Anabaptist Christianity?

Through repentance, Bible study, and openness to the Holy Spirit, early Anabaptists were transformed in their attitudes, beliefs, and lifestyles. The Holy Spirit caused them to be people of insight, courage, and effective witness. We conclude that an openness to the Holy Spirit was essential for an Anabaptist expression of faith and continues to be an important aspect of a unique Christian faith.

After discussing the questions that follow, you are invited in the final chapter to explore how you stand in relation to the core values, key questions, and signs of uniqueness in regard to Anabaptist faith.

## Questions for reflection and discussion

1. What new insights have you learned in regard to the Holy Spirit?

2. Discuss the following emphases to be found in various branches of the Christian faith.

| Many Christians emphasize: | Spirit-filled Christians emphasize: |
|---|---|
| Naturalistic, rational, and scientific reasoning. | Supernatural, revelational, and Spirit-led reasoning. |
| Being humanly enthusiastic and positive. | Being spiritually joyful and confident. |
| Working as if it all depends on oneself. | Working as if it all depends on God. |
| Letting one's life be the witness. | Being courageous in verbal witness. |

3. What might churches in the Global North learn from ministries in the Global South?

4. What might churches in the Global South learn from ministries in the Global North?

5. What will you do to open your life more fully to the Holy Spirit?

# ELEVEN

# Concluding Reflections on Anabaptist Essentials

*But as for you, continue in what you have learned
and firmly believed.*
*2 Timothy 3:14*

**I BEGAN** this study by saying that we can strengthen our Anabaptist beliefs without becoming competitive or hostile toward other points of view. We become stronger when we learn from each other. In these ten chapters I described what I believe are the essentials of the Christian faith from an Anabaptist perspective. They have been organized in relationship to three core values.

## What are the core values?

- *Jesus is the center of our faith.* Jesus is key to our understanding of Christianity, our interpretation of Scripture, and is the one to whom we give our ultimate allegiance.

- *Community is the center of our life.* Community becomes possible through horizontal forgiveness, is the context for discerning God's will, and often becomes most meaningful in small groups.

- *Reconciliation is the center of our work.* Reconciliation is central to establishing a relationship with God, to having harmonious personal relationships, and to serving as peacebuilders in a conflict-filled world.

The Holy Spirit is essential to the understanding, practice, and effectiveness of these three values.

## What are the key questions?

To summarize this study and to encourage dialogue, let me ask ten key questions and offer responses that recap the core values and essential teachings of Anabaptist faith.

*What is Christianity?* Christianity is not primarily a spiritual experience, a set of beliefs, or a one-time experience of forgiveness. Christianity is discipleship! It is following Jesus in daily life.

*How do we interpret Scripture?* Anabaptist Christians don't see the Bible as a flat book, as the history and fulfillment of Israel, or as primarily pointing to the sacrifice of Christ. The Scriptures are best interpreted from an ethical Christocentric point of view through the eyes and nature of Jesus.

*Who or what is our final authority?* Anabaptist believers don't blindly follow human orders, inner inclinations, or even every word of Scripture. Jesus is our final authority. He is Lord!

*What is essential for community?* While vertical forgiveness is essential for salvation, horizontal forgiveness is needed for community. The church is a forgiven and forgiving community of believers.

*How do we discern the will of God?* Both private meditation, on one hand, and being told what to think or do by authoritarian persons, on the other, are inadequate for discerning God's will. God's will is best discerned as Spirit-directed believers search the Scriptures and then give and receive counsel in the context of their community.

*How might we organize for community and accountability?* While many churches in North America are well organized and seek to serve through a variety of programs, this is not necessarily the best model. The early church and Anabaptist movement began in small groups, where members confronted each other and made each other strong enough to confront the world.

*How do we reconcile individuals to God?* Reconciliation with God may begin with an experience of forgiveness, but it takes a decision or series of decisions to leave past sins and loyalties for joyful obedience to Jesus Christ. Faith and obedience must stand together.

*How do we reconcile members to each other?* Neither overlooking sin nor treating wrongdoers with harsh criminal punishment is the Jesus way. Erring persons can be brought back to a relationship with Christ and the church through the rule of Christ and restorative justice.

*How do we reconcile conflicts in the world?* Meeting violence with violence generally leads to more violence. Followers of Christ are to overcome evil with good and to seek peace by working for justice. They are to bless those who persecute them. They must be willing to submit to punishment when they need to disobey a secular order that is contrary to following Jesus.

*What is essential for effectiveness?* Efficient organization, superior knowledge and skilled leadership are important but do not assure effectiveness. Effectiveness comes when followers of Christ allow the Holy Spirit to transform their thoughts, feelings, and actions.

## What are signs of a unique faith?

Following are ten signs of a unique Christian faith. Read the statements and place checkmarks by those that describe your understanding. If you find that these statements summarize your overall understandings of the Christian faith, consider yourself a Christian from an Anabaptist perspective.

_____ 1. I see Christianity as discipleship and seek to follow Jesus in daily life.

_____ 2. I interpret the Scriptures from an ethical Christocentric point of view.

_____ 3. I have accepted Jesus Christ as both my Lord and Savior.

_____ 4. I believe forgiveness is needed for both salvation and community.

_____ 5. I discern God's will through Bible study and the giving and receiving of counsel.

___ 6. I affirm that face-to-face groups are basic for accountability and a vital church.

___ 7. I believe transformation is the result of God's work and my responses to that work.

___ 8. I seek to resolve conflicts through mediation and the Rule of Christ.

___ 9. I reject all forms of violence and seek to overcome evil with good.

___ 10. I have publicly confessed my faith in Jesus and am experiencing the Holy Spirit in my life and ministry.

## A concluding blessing

May you be blessed with a firm faith and a charitable spirit as you share these essentials with those who are close to you and also with those who are distant. May you have the grace to refrain from falsely criticizing other points of view as you continue to strengthen and share your own.

# Notes

## Introduction

1   Harold S. Bender, "The Anabaptist Vision," in *The Recovery of the Anabaptist Vision*, ed. Guy F. Hershberger (Scottdale, PA: Herald Press, 1957), 29–54.

2   James C. Collins and Jerry I. Porras, "Building Your Company's Vision," *Harvard Business Review* 74, no. 5, (1996).

3   Jeff Wright was nurturing a dozen new fellowships to become rooted in Anabaptist thought and practice while serving as conference minister for the Pacific Southwest Mennonite Conference. See Stuart Murray, *The Naked Anabaptist: The Bare Essentials of a Radical Faith*, 5th anniv. ed. (Harrisonburg, VA: Herald Press, 2015); Alfred Neufeld, *What We Believe Together* (Intercourse, PA: Good Books, 2007); John D. Roth, *Beliefs: Mennonite Faith and Practice* (Scottdale, PA: Herald Press, 2005); and C. Arnold Snyder, *Anabaptist History and Theology*, rev. student ed. (Kitchener, ON: Pandora Press, 1997).

4   General Conference Mennonite Church and Mennonite Church, *Confession of Faith in a Mennonite Perspective* (Scottdale, PA: Herald Press, 1995).

## A Short History of Christianity

1   Alan Kreider, *The Change of Conversion and the Origin of Christendom* (Eugene, OR: Wipf & Stock, 2007), xiv–xvi.

2   For a biography of Constantine, see William Smith, ed., *A Dictionary of Christian Biography*, vol. 1 (New York: AMS Press, 1974), 623–49.

3   Murray, *Naked Anabaptist*, 62.

4   For an outline of Augustine's life and theology, see Erwin Fahlbusch, ed., *The Encyclopedia of Christianity*, vol. 1 (Grand Rapids, MI: Eerdmans, 1999), 159–65.

5   John D. Roth, *Stories: How Mennonites Came to Be* (Scottdale, PA: Herald Press, 2006). See chapter 2 for descriptions of revolt, reform, and renewal related to the Reformation.

6   Snyder, *Anabaptist History and Theology*, 114–17.

7   Walter Klaassen, *Anabaptism: Neither Catholic nor Protestant* (Kitchener, ON: Pandora Press, 2001), 24.

8   For further understanding on the various streams of Anabaptism, see Snyder, *Anabaptist History and Theology*, part B.

9   *Anabaptism: Neither Catholic nor Protestant* was first published in 1973 by Conrad Press. In 2001 it was revised and published as a third edition by Pandora Press, Kitchener, ON.

10  Paul M. Lederach, *A Third Way* (Scottdale, PA: Herald Press, 1980).

11  For primary sources related to themes that were important to the Anabaptists, see Walter Klaassen, ed., *Anabaptism in Outline* (Scottdale, PA: Herald Press, 1981).

12  Wilbert R. Shenk, "Why Missional and Mennonite Should Make Perfect Sense," in *Fully Engaged: Missional Church in an Anabaptist Voice*, ed. Stanley W. Green and James R. Krabill (Harrisonburg, VA: Herald Press, 2015), 21–22.

13  Bender, "The Anabaptist Vision," 29–30.

## Chapter 1

1   Kreider, *Change of Conversion*, xiv–xvi.

2   Theodore Runyon, *The New Creation: John Wesley's Theology Today* (Nashville: Abingdon Press, 1998), ch. 5.

3   J. I. Packer, interview with author, April 1991.

4   Doris Janzen Longacre, *Living More with Less*, 30th anniv. ed. (Harrisonburg, VA: Herald Press, 2010), 28–29.

5   Michele Hershberger, *God's Story, Our Story* (Harrisonburg, VA: Herald Press, 2013), 70–71.

6   Text drawn from David Augsburger, "The Mennonite Dream," *Gospel Herald* 70, no. 45 (1977), 855–56, reprinted from pamphlet #147, *The Mennonite Hour*.

7   César García, email message to author, February 5, 2016.

## Chapter 2

1    Sara Wenger Shenk, "Anabaptist Schools, Scripture and Spiritual Awakening," *The Mennonite*, November 13, 2015, https://themennonite.org/feature/anabaptist-schools-scripture-and-spiritual-awakening/.

2    Roth, *Beliefs: Mennonite Faith and Practice*, 38.

3    C. Arnold Snyder, *From Anabaptist Seed* (Kitchener, ON: Pandora Press, 1999), 12–13.

4    Klaassen, *Anabaptism in Outline*, 23–24, 72–73, 140ff.

5    Bruxy Cavey, "Walking in Receiving and Giving" (sermon, Mennonite World Conference Assembly, Harrisburg, PA, July 25, 2015).

6    Peter Kehler served as a missionary in Taiwan from 1959 to 1975 and from 1991 to 1993.

7    Ervin Stutzman, email message to author, January 31, 2016.

8    John Powell, email message to author, January 25, 2016.

9    Marion Bontrager, "Introduction to Biblical Literature," course Hesston (Kans.) College.

10   Gayle Gerber Koontz, "The Trajectory of Scripture and Feminist Conviction," *Conrad Grebel Review* 5, no. 3, (1987), 207.

11   Grace Holland, "Women in Ministry/Leadership in the Church," in *Windows to the Church: Selections from Twenty-Five Years of the Brethren in Christ History and Life*, ed. E. Morris Sider (Grantham, PA: Brethren in Christ Historical Society, 2003), 111.

12   Michele Hershberger, "Reading the Bible through a Missional Lens," in Green and Krabill, *Fully Engaged*, 180.

13   Quoted in Paul Schrag, "Claiborne: Make Holy Mischief," *Mennonite World Review*, February 29, 2016.

14   *Confession of Faith in a Mennonite Perspective*, 21–24.

## Chapter 3

1    Walter Wink, *The Powers That Be: Theology for a New Millennium* (New York: Doubleday, 1998), 39.

2    See especially chapter 6 in John D. Redekop, *Politics Under God* (Scottdale, PA: Herald Press, 2007).

3    Ibid., ch. 6.

## Chapter 4

1  Roberta Hestenes, lecture in the course "Building Christian Community through Small Groups" (Fuller Theological Seminary, Pasadena, CA, May 12–23, 1986).

2  Dietrich Bonhoeffer, *The Cost of Discipleship* (New York: Macmillan Publishing, 1961), 47.

3  Martin Luther King Jr., quoted on *USA Today Network*, January 18, 2016.

4  April Yamasaki, *Sacred Pauses: Spiritual Practices for Personal Renewal* (Harrisonburg, VA: Herald Press, 2013), 86–87.

5  Ken Sande, *The Peacemaker: A Biblical Guide to Resolving Personal Conflict* (Grand Rapids, MI: Baker Books, 1997), 109–19.

6  For further explanation of transactional and positional forgiveness, see ibid., 190.

7  The term *forgrieving* was coined by David Augsburger, faculty of Fuller Theological Seminary, Pasadena, California.

8  Suzanne Woods Fisher, *The Heart of the Amish: Life Lessons on Peacemaking and the Power of Forgiveness* (Grand Rapids, MI: Revell, 2015), 90.

9  Ibid., 23.

## Chapter 5

1  John H. Yoder, trans. and ed., *The Schleitheim Confession* (Scottdale, PA: Herald Press, 1973, 1977).

2  Information drawn from Michael Green's course "The Gospel of Matthew," Regent College, Vancouver, BC, 1988.

3  Byron Weber Becker, interview with author, May, 2016.

4  Jessica Reesor Rempel, correspondence with author, February 9, 2016.

5  John Powell, correspondence with author.

## Chapter 6

1  Takashi Yamada in discussion with author, July 1978.

2  William A. Beckham, *The Second Reformation: Reshaping the Church for the 21st Century* (Houston, TX: Touch Outreach Ministries, 1998), 25–26.

3  Reta Halteman Finger, *Of Widows and Meals: Communal Meals*

*in the Book of Acts* (Grand Rapids, MI: Eerdmans, 2007), 4–6.

4    Roberta Hestenes, "Definition of a Small Group: What Christian Small Groups Do" (lecture, Fuller Theological Seminary, Pasadena, CA, May 12, 1986).

5    Stutzman, email.

6    Conrad L. Kanagy, Tilahun Beyene, and Richard Showalter, *Winds of the Spirit: A Profile of Anabaptist Churches in the Global South* (Harrisonburg, VA: Herald Press, 2012), 59.

7    Ibid., 29.

### Chapter 7

1    Robert C. Solomon, *The Big Questions* (San Diego: HBJ Publishers, 1990), 47.

2    Snyder, *Anabaptist History and Theology*, 419.

3    Ibid., 87.

4    Ibid., 419.

5    Jim Wallis, *The Call to Conversion* (San Francisco: HarperOne, 2005), 4.

6    Myron S. Augsburger, introduction to *Probe: For an Evangelism That Cares*, ed. Jim Fairfield (Scottdale, PA: Herald Press, 1972), 7.

7    David Schroeder (1924–2015) was a highly respected professor of Bible at Canadian Mennonite Bible College, now Canadian Mennonite University, Winnipeg, MB.

8    Albert J. Wollen shared this diagram with me after leading a workshop on small groups at Peace Mennonite Church, Richmond, BC, in 1987.

9    Mennonite Church USA, "Desiring God's Coming Kingdom: A Missional Vision and Purposeful Plan for Mennonite Church USA" (Elkhart, IN: 2014), 3, http://mennoniteusa.org/wp-content/up-loads/2015/03/PurposefulPlan_2014Feb25.pdf.

10  Darren Petker, "Dying for Change," *Mennonite Brethren Herald*, December 2015, 19, http://mbherald.com/dying-for-change/.

11  Rick Warren, *The Purpose Driven Life* (Grand Rapids, MI: Zondervan, 2002), 183.

12  Willy Reimer, "Being a Denomination Led by the Holy Spirit," *Mennonite Brethren Herald*, March 1, 2014, http://mbherald.com/being-a-denomination-led-by-the-holy-spirit/.

13  Franklin Littell, *The Anabaptist View of the Church* (Boston, MA: Starr King Press, 1958), 1.

14  Hyoung Min Kim, *Sixteenth-Century Anabaptist Evangelism: Its Foundational Doctrines, Practices, and Impacts* (PhD dissertation, Southwestern Baptist Theological Seminary, 2001).

15  John K. Stoner, Jim Egli, and G. Edwin Bontrager, *Life to Share* (Scottdale, PA: Mennonite Publishing House, 1991), 27.

16  Hans Kasdorf, "Anabaptists and the Great Commission in the Reformation," *Mennonite Quarterly Review* 4, no. 2 (1975): 303–18.

17  Wolfgang Schaeufele, "The Missionary Vision and Activity of the Anabaptist Laity," *Mennonite Quarterly Review* 36 (1962): 99–115.

18  Probe '72, Minneapolis, MN, April 1972.

## Chapter 8

1  Rick Warren, *The Purpose Driven Church* 2nd ed., (Grand Rapids, MI: Zondervan, 2002), 158.

2  Walter Klaassen, *Living at the End of the Ages* (Lanham, MD: University Press of America, 1992), 211.

3  Modified from *Mediation and Facilitation Training Manual: Foundations and Skills for Constructive Conflict Transformation*, 4th ed. (Akron, PA: Mennonite Conciliation Service, 2000), 31–33.

4  Howard Zehr, *The Little Book of Restorative Justice* (New York: Good Books, 2015), 6.

5  *Minister's Manual*, ed. John Rempel (Scottdale, PA: Herald Press, 1998).

6  *Hymnal: A Worship Book* (Scottdale, PA: Mennonite Publishing House, 1992), no. 777.

7  Murray, *Naked Anabaptist*, 122–23.

8  Marlin Jeschke, *Discipling in the Church: Recovering a Ministry of the Gospel* (Scottdale, PA: Herald Press, 1988), 16.

9  Stutzman, correspondence with the author.

## Chapter 9

1  Cavey, "Walking in Receiving and Giving."

2  Ervin R. Stutzman, *From Nonresistance to Justice: The Transformation of Mennonite Church Peace Rhetoric 1908–2008* (Scottdale, PA: Herald Press, 2011), 284.

3    Dietrich Bonhoeffer, *Ethics* (New York: Touchstone Books, 1955), 79.

4    Murray, *Naked Anabaptist*, 151.

5    James C. Juhnke and Carol M. Hunter, *The Missing Peace: The Search for Nonviolent Alternatives in United States History* (Kitchener, ON: Pandora Press, 2004).

6    Murray, *Naked Anabaptist*, 150.

7    Snyder, *From Anabaptist Seed*, 42, 44.

8    See the PBS film by Gary Weimberg and Catherine Ryan, *Soldiers of Conscience* (American Documentary, Inc., 2008), www.pbs.org/pov/soldiersofconscience.

9    Ronald J. Sider, *Nonviolent Action: What Christian Ethics Demands but Most Christians Have Never Really Tried* (Grand Rapids, MI: Brazos Press, 2015), xiii.

10   Gene Sharp, *Politics of Nonviolent Action*, vol. 2 (Boston, MA: Porter Sargent, 1973).

11   Sider, *Nonviolent Action*, xv.

12   Ibid., 146–50.

13   Sarah Thompson, "Moving Toward Conflict and the Beloved Community," *The Mennonite*, January 18, 2016, https://themennonite.org/moving-towards-conflict-and-the-beloved-community/.

14   Pope Paul VI, "Message of His Holiness for the Celebration of the Day of Peace," January 1, 1972.

15   Bonnie Price Lofton, "Oakland Youth Transformed by Restorative Justice Practices," *The Mennonite*, May 27, 2015, https://themennonite.org/daily-news/oakland-youth-transformed-by-restorative-justice-practices/.

16   "Brief History of Conscientious Objection," last modified November 2007, https://www.swarthmore.edu/library/peace/conscientiousobjection/co%20website/pages/HistoryNew.htm.

17   Palmer Becker, "I Was Ready to Fight," *Our Faith Mennonite Digest* (Spring 2004), 9.

18   Additional examples include BIC Compassionate Ministries of Zambia, Mennonite Brethren Development Organization of India, Mennonite Diakonia Service of Indonesia, Korea Anabaptist Center, Christlicher Dienst of Germany, Centro Cristiano para Justicia of Colombia, Mennonite Central Committee Canada, Mennonite Central Committee U.S., and Mennonite Disaster Service.

19   Laura Kalmar, "The God-Bearing Life . . . of a Magazine," *Mennonite Brethren Herald*, June 2015, 4.

**Chapter 10**

1   J. B. Toews, "Spiritual Renewal," in *The Witness of the Holy Spirit: Proceedings of the Eighth Mennonite World Conference*, ed. Cornelius J. Dyck (Elkhart, IN: Mennonite World Conference, 1967), 56–63.

2   Peter Klassen, "The Anabaptist View of the Holy Spirit," *Mennonite Life* 23, no. 1 (1968): 27–31.

3   Klaassen, *Living at the End of the Ages*, ch. 4.

4   Menno Simons, *Complete Writings of Menno Simons*, trans. John Funk (Elkhart, IN: 1870), 496.

5   Walter Klaassen, "Spiritualization in the Reformation," *Mennonite Quarterly Review* 37 (1963), 67–77.

6   Richard J. Foster, *Celebration of Discipline: The Path to Spiritual Growth* (New York: Harper & Row, 1978), 5.

7   Statistics were derived from combining the findings of Kanagy, Beyene, and Showalter as reported in *Winds of the* Spirit with those reported by Mennonite World Conference in *World Directory, 2015*.

8   David Wiebe, review of Kanagy, Beyene, and Showalter, *Winds of the Spirit*, Mennonite Brethren Herald, January 1, 2013.

9   Arthur Duck, "Exuberance for the Spirit: Acts 2 from a Brazilian Perspective," *Mennonite Brethren Herald*, June 1, 2011.

# The Author

**PALMER BECKER** has served the church as a pastor, church planter, missionary, conference executive, author, and educator. A graduate of Goshen College, Anabaptist Mennonite Biblical Seminary, Regent College, and Fuller Theological Seminary, Becker most recently served as director of the Hesston College pastoral ministries program. His booklet *What Is an Anabaptist Christian?* has been translated into twenty languages. Palmer and his wife, Ardys, live in Kitchener, Ontario, and are members of Waterloo North Mennonite Church. They have four grown children.